Love

THE ART OF LIVING SERIES

Series Editor: Mark Vernon

From Plato to Bertrand Russell philosophers have engaged wide audiences on matters of life and death. *The Art of Living* series aims to open up philosophy's riches to a wider public once again. Taking its lead from the concerns of the ancient Greek philosophers, the series asks the question "How should we live?". Authors draw on their own personal reflections to write philosophy that seeks to enrich, stimulate and challenge the reader's thoughts about their own life.

Love

Tony Milligan

ACUMEN

Acumen Publishing Limited
4 Saddler Street
Durham
DH1 3NP
www.acumenpublishing.co.uk

ISBN: 978-1-84465-506-9

British Library Cataloguing-in-Publication Data
A catalogue record for this book is available from the British Library.

Typeset in Warnock Pro.
Printed by Ashford Colour Press Ltd, UK.

For Betty and Jack Milligan, my parents

Contents

Acknowledgements   viii

1. Introduction   1

2. Doubts about love   9

3. The depth of love   29

4. A sense of worth   51

5. Togetherness and loss   73

6. Irreplaceability   95

7. What can we love?   116

Further reading   139
References   141
Index   143

Acknowledgements

The account of intimacy that is set out in the following pages owes a good deal to a series of discussions held with Christian Maurer and Kamila Pacovská during the time when we were postgraduates at the University of Glasgow and were covertly using departmental rooms during the evenings. The account of irreplaceability owes a good deal to the students who took part in my "Theories of Love" seminar at the University of Aberdeen between 2007 and 2009 and to constructive comments made by a patient and gentle audience at the "Reasons of Love" conference at the University of Leuven in the summer of 2011. The account of grief and loss draws on previous work on false emotions and on discussions with impressive and capable students on the Applied Ethics course I taught during my term at the University of Hull in 2010. The team at Acumen has helped to move the book on at a pace. Careful editing by Kate Williams has improved the text, series editor Mark Vernon offered important guidance at an early stage and Steven Gerrard has repeatedly injected enthusiasm and has helped give structure to the process. The largest debt of all is to my wife, Suzanne, without whom my understanding of love would be in every way diminished.

1. Introduction

Love can be several splendid things, a source of joy and gladness, a support or a consolation or a wonderful surprise. But it can also be a source of unease, of fruitless longing and regret. We may be harmed by love, harmed by loving and perhaps even harmed by the love of another. Love does us no good when we love the wrong person. If such love is reciprocated (and perhaps *especially* if it is reciprocated) it can lead us to waste the best years of our lives. It may lead us to lose our chance of contentment without in any way adding to the well-being of the person that we love. Similarly, we may love someone who *could* make us happy if they were to love us in return but they do not do so. Our love may be unreciprocated and yet it may stubbornly refuse to go away. Under such circumstances, love can be little more than a subtle form of self-laceration. These considerations may lead us to accept that love does not conquer all.

In spite of such drawbacks, and in spite of the difficulties of loving someone suitable and doing so in the right way, we are creatures who need to love and who need to be loved. This is a claim that shapes a good deal of what follows. Another claim that helps to give shape to this book is that sexualized and intimate love of the sort that often exists between partners and spouses is a good exemplar of love of any kind. Although I write about love in general, about parental love and about the love of neighbours, it is love of this sort that is the main focus of my attention. It is a love that is sometimes regarded with suspicion, partly because it is sexualized and partly because it involves a special attachment to the exclusion of all others.

One familiar charge against sexualized and intimate love is that, in some unavoidable way, it is too grasping and too selfish. It may then be tempting to regard it as a poor model for love in general and to look elsewhere for the latter, to the love that is built into friendship, to the love of unselfish parents, or to love that is a gratuitous gift to our neighbours. A rather different, but equally familiar, charge is that sexualized intimate love is (again unavoidably) delusional and requires an overestimation of the person we love. Why else would we single them out if not because we regard them (delusionally) as uniquely and supremely beautiful, accomplished or charming?

Such doubts (which may also apply to a greater or lesser degree to any other love) are instances of what I shall call "pessimism about the nature of love" or more simply "pessimism about love". For the pessimist, it is not simply the case that *sometimes* love is delusional or shaped by egocentricity, or that it tends towards overestimation during some initial and perhaps romantic stage. Rather, for the pessimist, love (of whatever sort they regard with suspicion) is *always and unavoidably* delusional or compromised by our human egocentricity and cannot escape from being so compromised. The oversights and delusions that can sometimes accompany love are taken by the pessimist to be characteristic of the kind of love that they wish to place in doubt. On such a view, the fact that someone loves another person tells us more about them than it does about the person they love. And what it tells us is far from flattering.

Through an exploration of some obvious, and some not so obvious, features of love (features that stand in sharp relief in the case of sexualized love), I shall try to defuse such pessimism. And here I do mean "defuse" rather than directly confront. I shall not pretend to have a knock-down argument against it. Instead, I shall try to show, in a steady and piecemeal manner, that pessimism about the nature of love involves a limited and distorted picture of love, a picture that is based on what happens on those occasions when love fails or when it goes wrong. I take this gradual approach because of the involved nature of the subject and also because pessimism about love can be motivated and supported by doubt of another and more personal sort. This other kind of doubt may not be removed simply by accepting that love *can* be warm, generous and truthful. It may even be made worse by such an acceptance.

What I allude to here is a kind of doubt that I shall call "scepticism about being loved". The sceptic about being loved cannot accept that they are loved in a genuine or authentic manner. Many of us have, at one time or another, suffered from scepticism of this sort. It is a familiar predicament. Any one of us may come to believe that we have good reasons for doubting another's declared love for us. But at the same time we may remain sensitive to the possibility that, in spite of our doubts, the love in question may still be genuine. One circumstance that gives rise to such a sceptical predicament is the fact that love does not always turn out the way that we imagine. It does not always take the form that we have expected or come from a source that we have anticipated. Another, and perhaps more obvious, circumstance that may give rise to scepticism about being loved is self-doubt. At the back of our minds a question may always linger: "Why would such a person love me?" or, even worse, "Why would anyone love me?"

In the opening chapter I shall suggest, and *up to a point* try to show, that pessimism about the nature of love and scepticism about being loved can feed off one another. Operating together or in sequence, either kind of doubt can hamper our best attempts to live well. They can prevent us from accepting that we love and prevent us from fully embracing the possibility that we may be loved in return. But, considered on their own separate merits, these doubts are not always equally misleading. Whereas pessimism about the nature of love is ultimately based on a distorted view of what love must involve, and should never therefore be endorsed, scepticism about being loved is not always misplaced. There are occasions on which others seem to love us, declare that they love us and believe that they love us, but nonetheless they do not do so. Under such circumstances, doubting the love of the other person may be the best and most realistic option. By way of a contrast, there are other occasions on which scepticism *is* misplaced. It is also true that any serial scepticism, carried from relationship to relationship, may deprive us of the chance to see ourselves in the light of another's love. Openness to the possibility that we may be loved is an important human virtue that is incompatible with such a serial scepticism.

My sampling of arch-pessimists in the opening chapter will include Freud, Schopenhauer and Proust. One thing they share is the conviction that although love is delusional it is also "deep". Chapter 2 will explore this important idea of the depth of love and will suggest that love's depth is at least partly a matter of its connection to our shared human need to live a life that is well motivated and to acknowledge our own worth. On the one hand, *loving* gives order and structure to our world, it shapes our everyday actions and our attitudes towards those things we regard as important. On the other hand, *being loved* is bound up with the recognition of our own value.

Chapter 3 will attempt to show that our sense of self-worth cannot rest solely on the fact that we are autonomous rational agents. We need to accept that we are or have been loved, and that we remain lovable, in order to see ourselves in a realistic manner, as the valuable beings that we are. However there remains the possibility that our need to be loved may be accepted in combination with a restricted pessimism about the nature of love. It remains a possibility that someone may accept that love is egocentric or delusional (or that *some* kinds of love such as sexualized intimate love have this drawback) while claiming that there is a special kind of love that is exempt from the problem. A well-known example of such exception-building is Anders Nygren's rejection of erotic love in favour of a restricted and problematic account of Christian love. But if pessimism about the nature of love, and more especially about intimate love, is ultimately misplaced, this is an exception we do not need. Furthermore, Christian love may be understood in a more attractive and less restrictive manner that involves a rejection of any pessimism about the nature of love and instead embraces the idea that all kinds of love (including sexualized intimate love) can have a praiseworthy spiritual dimension. Even so, a modified conception of Christian love may still remain associated with the problematic view that neighbourly love can be extended outwards in all directions and that we are all equally suitable recipients. I regard this as problematic because it is not obvious that we *ought* to love everyone or that all humans *are* lovable. There may be some humans whose actions place them beyond the reach of a reasonable and defensible love. Part of the reason for this is that any kind of love for other humans involves the desire that their lives should go well, or at least the desire that they should come to no great harm. In the case of humans who are guilty of evil beyond vice, such a desire may be inappropriate.

Love of other humans not only involves the desire that their lives go well: it also involves a binding of our own well-being to theirs. This is particularly clear in the case of sexualized intimate love. Such love emerges out of our nature as humans, and it emerges out of our shared need to be loved. As a brief summary, sexualized love, like any other kind of love, involves *seeing*, *wanting* and *needing*. But while this claim can be given support, and may be expanded on in various ways, it does not generalize out into a complete theory of everything that we are inclined to call "love". Nor does it give us the fundamental building blocks for such a theory. Readers may therefore find that what follows is more systematic than a cluster of comments but less systematic than a comprehensive account. This limitation has less to do with the available space than it has to do with love itself. While we may explore all sorts of important features of love, and do so in illuminating and interesting ways, love remains, in some respects, mysterious. Recognition of this allows us to understand another sense in which love is deep. It is deep in the sense that it is *up to a point* unfathomable.

Chapter 4 will examine the themes of togetherness and loss. I shall suggest that sexualized intimate love involves more than a desire for the well-being of the other *plus* a sexual desire for (or a sexual relationship with) them. But this is not because sex is irrelevant to intimacy. Rather, there is something about sexual togetherness and the sharing of pleasures that can exemplify the sharing of a life. In turn, what is involved in the sharing of a life is best understood by considering what it is like to lose, and to grieve for, someone we love. On occasions of loss we recognize, all too readily, that our own well-being and that of the person we have lost have become entangled. Understanding this goes to the heart of what intimacy involves.

Chapter 5 considers another aspect of the experience of loss. Part of what makes grief so difficult is the recognition that those we love are irreplaceable. But it is a mistake to imagine that we must understand this important idea by appeal to the delusion that our loved one is not only beautiful but *uniquely* beautiful, *uniquely* accomplished, charming or in possession of physical, behavioural or even spiritual properties that nobody else could match. Instead, what makes any human irreplaceable is their relation to the past. After all, we do not want to go home to copies, clones or duplicates of our loved ones. Rather, we want to go home to the loved ones with whom we have a shared history. In my own case, I want to go home to the Suzanne that I met at the end of my teens and who sat out with me under the stars. A duplicate just wouldn't do. Once irreplaceability is understood in this way, there is no need to appeal to a special kind of overestimation in order to make sense of love. We can see those we love as the remarkable beings that they are, as beings with whom we have an important personal connection. We can love them just as they are and for what they are while still regarding them as unique.

The final chapter expands the scope of the enquiry to consider the bounds or limits of love. It poses a simple question: "What can we love?" In response, I suggest that we can love anything that we can grieve over. Where there is no place for the possibility of grief, there is also no place for the possibility of love. I have taken this as one of the ways in which an understanding of sexualized intimate love can inform our understanding of love of any sort, including the love of non-human creatures and the love of non-sentient things such as forests and familiar places. Grief over the loss of other creatures and other things is a real possibility. We can love them and we can do so in life-enriching ways that will leave us vulnerable to their loss. I shall also suggest that we should be more open to the possibilities of this kind of love and that we do not love enough.

Nevertheless, just so long as we regard the importance of the past and the possibility of grief as fundamental, it will be difficult to allow that we can, in any genuine and straightforward sense, love strangers. We may be able to love our neighbours and acquaintances, should we feel so inclined, but loving strangers is a quite different matter. We can, and ought to, do various things to show hospitality and to welcome the stranger in our midst. We can also show them due respect. But in the absence of a shared past *of the relevant sort*, we cannot love them. The shared past in question cannot, for example, simply reduce to our belonging to the same species or our sharing a connection to a broader evolutionary or social history. An interesting corollary of the fact that we cannot love strangers is that "love at first sight" is not possible *if it is understood in the strictest sense*. It is not my intention to suggest that talk about such love is misguided. Such talk can and often does track something. But what it tracks is the sudden beginnings of love's emergence and not an instant love. A further corollary is that, although there are some humans who we ought not to love and others who we simply cannot love, there are nonetheless non-human creatures, things and places that we can and ought to love. Pessimism about the nature of love for the non-human is no more helpful and realistic than pessimism about the nature of sexualized intimate love.

2. Doubts about love

Love is deeply bound up with our humanity. It is also available in various shapes and sizes. There is the sustained, erotic and sexualized love that we can have for a partner; the transitory romantic love that idealizes its object; the love that is part of friendship; the parental and filial love that may exist between mother or father and child; the love of a sister or brother; love of the family dog; love of neighbours, of mankind, of the planet, of all living things and so on. Some of these loves have their own specialized terminology of *philia*, *agape*, *eros* and *caritas*, a terminology that has been passed on to us from antiquity.

Of these different kinds of love, it is love of the sustained, erotic and sexualized sort that will be my primary focus, the love that we may have for a particular individual with whom we want to share our life and our bed. At the best of times, this love can be a source of pleasure, joy and a lightness of spirit. When it fails, ends or is unrequited it can be a source of deep unhappiness. Often it brings a mixture of pleasure, longing and loss into our lives and those who have experienced it will readily understand what I mean by saying that it can involve the whole of our being. I shall refer to it as "sexualized intimate love" and occasionally, for simplicity, as "sexualized love". I will also take it as a good model for love of any sort. In what follows you may safely assume that, unless otherwise stated, I shall always have this love in mind. The decision to focus on love that is sexualized, rather than friendship love or a love of humanity, no doubt says something about my own life and about my own philosophical temperament. But I also hope to show that the approach is a good one and that we have strong reasons to reject longstanding suspicions and doubts about sexualized intimate love, doubts that may hinder our best efforts to live well and to be content.

Two kinds of doubt

When any one of us loves someone, in whatever way, we see them as special or unique. On an optimistic account, we recognize what we might otherwise miss. We see more of what there is to be seen. However, it is easy to appreciate the merits of a less optimistic attitude, an attitude that I shall call "pessimism about the nature of love". For the pessimist, love of some specified sort, or love of any sort whatsoever, is blind in the sense of delusional. It *unavoidably* involves an inability to see things as they are. On such an account, when we love someone we tend to overlook their shortcomings and underestimate their faults; we project a whole series of imagined properties onto them, properties they do not, and perhaps never will, possess. Nobody else may seem so witty, pretty and important. But, for the pessimist, the wit, the allure and the importance are only present in the eye of the beholder. Others do not see these wonderful qualities for the simple reason that they are not there.

Sexualized intimate love, with its insistence on the special standing or the uniqueness of the other, is often taken to involve delusions of just this sort. Why else would we regard others as special or unique if not because of imagined properties and accomplishments? For the pessimist, love unsettles our ability to make good and sensible judgements. Even worse, the delusions that a sexualized love involves may turn out to be temporary. Were we able to sustain them indefinitely we might live in a blissful ignorance. But life may not be so kind. After an initial rush of enthusiasm for the other (the time of romance and of falling in love) we may come with greater or lesser speed to recognize that the person we love is quite ordinary. Separation, divorce or a sustained disappointment may then ensue. At best (or worst) there may be a dull mutual acceptance based on recognition that we have disappointed them just as they have disappointed us. In this way, pessimism about the nature of love, and more particularly about the nature and merits of sexualized love, may not identify our own predicament as anything special or unique, but nonetheless it can feed into doubts of a very personal sort.

In particular, it can feed into, and be reinforced by, another form of doubt that I shall call "scepticism about being loved". We may or may not believe that love, or more especially sexualized love, is intrinsically delusional, but either way we can question whether we are its recipients. Personal insecurities can make us ready to believe the worst. Knowing what we do about ourselves, we may wonder how anyone could genuinely come to love us. And while the doubts that are involved in such scepticism may not rule out relationships or marriage, success in establishing and sustaining such convenient arrangements need not be taken as conclusive evidence that scepticism about being loved is misplaced. The other person may simply have settled for what they can get. The benefits of companionship, under circumstances of mutual disappointment, may even convince two individuals to stay together despite the fact that the benefits do not match up to what we have all hoped for in our more optimistic moments.

Personal doubts about the genuineness of someone's love may also persist in the face of the obvious fact that most of us *have* been loved, and loved in an utterly genuine but different way, by our parents. Although when I suggest this I am assuming that the reader has largely overcome their childhood doubts about being loved, doubts that can form a point of origin for all sorts of subsequent anxieties. Our earliest fears and worries about such matters may become deeply sedimented in a way that feeds into later uncertainty. But even for those who have managed to leave childhood doubts where they belong, there is a sense in which parental love comes too easily. With a partner or spouse, love is, or may seem to be, earned or in some way achieved. And because of this, their attitude towards us carries an authority that parental judgements lack. When we are fortunate enough to find love, we come to share our lives with a particular individual not by dint of being born into a relationship with them but because they have impressed us and we have impressed them (although we may each be hard pushed to explain exactly what it is that makes our loved one special). Those we love in an intimate and sexualized manner also come to share our adult lives in a way that parents do not. There is a serious danger that they may find out who we are. They may discover all sorts of awkward truths that we would ordinarily conceal. And because of this, the claims of a partner or spouse to love us "just as we are", or "warts and all", may seem too good to be true. And sometimes they are.

This is not to say that we must doubt the honesty or sincerity of those who say that they love us. Instead, we may simply doubt their self-knowledge. It is perfectly possible for someone to confuse a vague sense that they *ought* to love us, or that they *must* love us, with the belief that they actually do so. There are, after all, plausible imitations of love, false loves of various sorts that can sometimes convince just as readily as the real thing. This applies not only in the case of sexualized love but also in the case of other kinds of love. It applies even when we might think it easy to tell the difference between real love and any imitation. Consider the claims of love (albeit love of a different sort) made by long-standing religious devotees who insist that they love their god. I will take it that such a love may be genuine or that it may initially be genuine and then erode into something else. An individual devotee may gradually awaken to a sense of sadness or yearning for all that they have given up in the name of their love. But even in the face of this sense of loss and personal incompleteness they may still firmly believe in the authenticity of their love. Nothing that we say may shake their conviction. But the strength of such conviction can derive from the fact that the alternative may seem utterly unbearable. In the lives of a couple, where the belief in love's genuineness may be shared, and in the absence of any tell-tale sadness and yearning, a false love may look even more convincing.

Scepticism about being loved, and about being loved as we want to be loved, is a form of doubt that may alternate with doubt of the first kind: doubt about the nature of love. Nonetheless, there is, or at least there can be, a tension between the two. Sometimes, and perhaps often, those who suffer from scepticism about being loved assume that love itself is *not* intrinsically delusional and that others are to be envied for enjoying something real and wonderful. But although scepticism about being loved and pessimism about the nature of love may occasionally be in tension, they have a common root in the belief that a deeply desirable condition is withheld from us or is simply unavailable. Because of this, each doubt may play off the other.

Even so, scepticism about being loved is personal in a way that pessimism about the nature of love is not. And this consideration shapes familiar philosophical treatments of love that in some way or other have a background preference for the impersonal. Scepticism about being loved (in a sexualized manner or otherwise) tends to drop out of view, as if it were beyond the scope of philosophy. There is a large philosophical literature concerning pessimism about the nature of love but very little on this more personal form of doubt. Plato is a partial exception here, as almost everywhere else. In his earliest dialogue on love, the *Lysis*, he shows a keen appreciation of how doubts about being loved can establish themselves at an early stage in our lives, in our relations with our parents. In this dialogue, Socrates speaks to two young men, and quickly shakes their assumption that their parents already have a *reason* to love them. Instead, he suggests that "everyone will love you and be on familiar terms with you if you become knowledgeable, because you'll be helpful and beneficial, but if you don't, no one will love you – not your father, nor your mother, nor your relatives, nor anyone else for that matter" (*Lysis* 210d). In spite of the upbeat tone of the dialogue, this is a disturbing episode and we may wonder whether anything of this sort ever really happened. Some queries are a little too unsettling.

Although sometimes overshadowed by his subsequent writings on love, the *Lysis* is a dialogue in which Plato seems to have a head start on Freud. It acknowledges the desire to be loved as an ordinary human desire. Freud tends instead to treat it as part of the make-up of women. Men, by contrast, on successive Freudian accounts need to love. But in Plato's other dialogues dealing with love the priority of loving is generally re-established and the importance of being loved tends to drop out of the picture. For attempts to give a more fundamental standing to the latter, we need to look elsewhere, and in particular to the work of post-Freudians such as John Bowlby, who regard our capacity to love, and to maintain mental health, as not so much a skill but rather a pattern that is stamped on us by our early experience of being loved by a parent, specifically a mother or a substitute mother. Using an embryological analogy, Bowlby suggests that we need maternal care just as the tissues of the embryo need contact with an appropriate "organizer" (1951: 53). Whatever we make of attempts to understand the importance of being loved in such clinical terms, they at least involve recognition that it is a key and necessary human experience. And they do not shy away from the problems of being loved because they fall on the wrong side of a supposed divide between what is manly and what is weak, feminine and insecure.

Another concern about being loved is that it touches a raw nerve. Perplexity about whether or not we are loved is deeply personal in a way that often seems alien to philosophy, or at least alien to a familiar way of doing philosophy that remains blind to the personal and separated off from the art of living. At the expense of a little overgeneralizing, I am tempted to say that philosophy allows us to address our most fundamental concerns but on occasions it does so in an indirect manner. There are times when it works by a sideways step, by a process of deflection or re-description. Distressing issues that strike at the very heart of our lives, and cast doubt on our habitual practices, are often reframed until they appear to concern something less intimate, such as the human condition in a general sense, or the nature of love in a sense that is equally general and emphatically impersonal. In the process, questions such as "How do I know that I am loved?" can be overlooked or set aside as if they were questions that we can ask only when we are not doing philosophy. We may even become convinced that the only philosophically significant task is one that involves finding the best definition of love and the best hierarchical system of classification into erotic or sexualized love, Christian love, romantic love and so on.

While classification, definition and comparison *are* philosophically significant tasks they are not the only such tasks that we may attempt to carry out. Sometimes philosophy and philosophical discussions of life can involve a more personal dimension and even a more personal mode of reflection. Sometimes the personal and the impersonal do not conveniently fall apart. I want to suggest that deliberation about sexualized love is just such a case. We always relate it to our own circumstances.

The interplay between pessimism and scepticism

There has never been a shortage of pessimists about the nature of love and especially about sexualized intimate love. Such pessimism surfaces in philosophical and related discourses but also in the lives of individuals who find themselves in some way disappointed. They may look to a theory about love in order to make sense of a personal predicament. Consider the case of Prince Charles and Princess Diana. When asked by an interviewer about whether or not they loved one another, Diana replied, "Of course", but Charles tagged on the ill-advised qualification, "whatever love means": unfortunate words that captured a sense of personal disillusionment exquisitely well. In retrospect this was not a good beginning. We may even wonder why, at the time, Diana did not recognize that these were the words of someone who did not love her rather than, more innocently, the words of an uncomfortable man with little taste for showing his feelings in public.

We need not regard Charles's pessimism about the nature of love, or the scepticism about being loved that Diana could have entertained, as forms of the hardest-headed realism, although they may both appear realistic because we know how the story of Charles and Diana ends. The same is not true of other and less-well-documented attempts by couples to build a life together. It is not, for example, true in my own case. I write in the firm belief that my love for my wife, Suzanne, is real and in the anticipation that it will continue, and also in the belief that it is reciprocated and in the hope that it will remain so. But repeated disappointments may lead any of us to generalize from our own case and to embrace some form of pessimism about love itself, and in doing so we may embrace the consoling thought that while we are not loved in the way storybooks describe, this is because the love we desire exists only in storybooks and otherwise forms no part of the real world. An epiphany or sudden shock to the system, administered by the realization that a long-trusted love may be a sham, can have much the same effect. Consider the impact of one such shock as it is depicted in James Joyce's short story "The Dead". The central character, Gabriel, has spent the evening at a dinner party held by his aunts. His task was to give the after-dinner speech. Later, his wife

Gretta tells him of a lost love, a boy from the gasworks who loved her and died, she believes, for her sake.

> While he had been full of memories of their secret life together, full of tenderness and joy and desire, she had been comparing him in her mind with another. A shameful consciousness of his own person assailed him. He saw himself as a ludicrous figure, acting as a penny-boy for his aunts, a nervous well-meaning sentimentalist, orating to vulgarians, and idealizing on his own clownish lusts, the pitiable fellow he had caught a glimpse of in the mirror. (1992: 221)

How consoling it would be in such a situation to cover over this shame with the thought that Gretta has been pining only after some childish ideal of love and that he, Gabriel, is more grown-up about such matters. But the impact of the revelation on Gabriel is so devastating precisely because he still believes in love and in the possibility of the kind of love that Gretta has apparently lost.

A sceptic about being loved – someone such as Gabriel after his moment of epiphany – may find that their scepticism threatens their sense of self-worth. But when such scepticism is coupled with a broader and more impersonal pessimism about the nature of love, the combination grants a degree of protection against suspicions that something real, better and above all available eludes us. Such a combination may even allow us to imagine that we are in some way above the folly of others. It may be tempting to go for full life cover and to embrace *both* scepticism and pessimism. But what if the scepticism is misplaced and we close ourselves off to a love that is utterly genuine? After all, while anyone may doubt the authenticity of another's love, most of us are not in the position of Gabriel, or, for that matter, Diana.

Similarly, pessimism about the nature of love is not obviously more realistic than the doubt of someone who cannot accept that they are loved. If the pessimists are right and love is systematically delusional then surely it would be possible to tell some background story about humans that would help us to understand just why this is the case. But attempts to tell such a story are often crudely reductionist and difficult to believe. Of these, one of the more impressive is Arthur Schopenhauer's treatment of love as the way in which nature dupes us into producing the next generation. Part of what is attractive about a pessimism that sets itself out in this way is its play on the idea that we love because of the kinds of creatures that we are.

In Schopenhauer's case, there is a clear autobiographical element to his pessimism about love. He stayed unmarried but not by choice. It was, rather, the result of a desperate lack of success in a series of romantic entanglements. While still a student at Göttingen, Schopenhauer fell in love with Karoline Jagermann, the mistress of the Duke of Weimar, but she was, from the standpoint of polite society, out of his league. The love was not reciprocated. He subsequently stumbled from encounter to encounter, fathering a child with a woman in Dresden before moving on to an intense affair with a multiply entangled but rather attractive young opera singer in Berlin. The affair having petered out, he immersed himself for a time in his writing and turned to the company of pets. Schopenhauer never entirely escaped from a deep longing for a sexualized love and for someone with whom he could share his life. In his mid forties, he proposed marriage but was again, and we may think wisely, rejected by a seventeen-year-old girl, Flora Weiss. His later essay *On Women* (1851) bears the stamp of these successive disappointments. It is unpleasant to the point of misogyny:

> Nature has not destined them, as the weaker sex, to be dependent on strength but on cunning; this is why they are instinctively crafty, and have an ineradicable tendency to lie. For as lions are furnished with claws and teeth, elephants with

tusks, boars with fangs, bulls with horns, and the cuttlefish
with its dark, inky fluid, so Nature has provided woman for
her protection and defence with the faculty of dissimulation,
and all the power which Nature has given to man in the form
of bodily strength and reason has been conferred on woman
in this form.   (1970: 83)

Here we see a combination of pessimism about love and a
general case for men to be on their guard. Women, and presum-
ably the women in his own past, have pretended and deceived.
The conclusion to be drawn is that when the male of the species
sees someone who holds out the promise of happiness he stands
in need of a reminder that this is just nature's way of getting things
done: "Nature can attain her end only by implanting in the individual a certain *delusion*, and by virtue of this, that which in truth
is merely a good thing for the species seems to him a good thing
for himself" (1958: vol. II, 538). For Schopenhauer, we are all driven
to reproduce with a biologically appropriate partner. Having found
someone who appears to be a suitable mate we are duped into
seeing them as unique and as a fountain of beauty and charm, or at
least we are so duped until we have performed our biological duty.
Our task done, the scales then fall from our eyes and love comes
to an end.

Schopenhauer's remedy for nature's little conspiracy involves a
precautionary recognition of the danger before it is too late. But,
for those who have already been duped, those like Diana, Gabriel
and, on numerous occasions, Schopenhauer, there is the consoling
thought that nobody else fares any better. Love makes fools of us
all. The trick is simply to limit the damage. This charmingly simple
pessimism, the reduction of love to a combination of deliberate
deception (by women) and unconscious urges (implanted in both
men and women) is specifically concerned with sexualized love and,
unless embellished with additional clauses, it fails to make sense of

such love in cases where the love exists between members of the same sex, between individuals who manifestly cannot breed. It is also more controversial than the observation, now commonplace, that there must be an evolutionary tale to tell about love. Mixing biological insight and a mystical conception of a dark, unconscious *Will*, Schopenhauer claims that nature has imbued us not only with the capacity to love but also with a strong disposition to do so. But even if this were the case, it would still not follow that such a disposition *must* operate by means of delusion. After all, why would we need to be misled when we could just as easily have evolved a natural disposition to respond to real properties? This would seem to be a simpler, and less demanding, way for nature to get things done.

On Schopenhauer's approach there are two principal reasons for rejecting this option. The first reason is a broad conviction that we are at the mercy of unconscious life forces that are not only beyond our control but are also, to some extent, beyond our understanding. A lucid and rational account of evolutionary advantages and disadvantages will only ever scratch the surface of what is going on. The second reason is a broad pessimism about humans and about human existence, a conviction that living entails suffering and that the suffering in question is driven by our desires. This conception of desire as self-frustrating is reminiscent of a popular Western understanding of Buddhism. It can also be softened in various ways and may be placed within a warm concern for all those caught up in the resulting human predicament. But even when softened in this way, it still dovetails with the view that love *has to be* delusional because if we knew that sexualized intimate love was going to disappoint we would all remain single and unattached, a state of affairs that the dark, unconscious forces in our lives would not deem acceptable.

While we may allow that the unconscious is a real influence, that it is *to some extent* dark, and that love is somewhat mischievous, Schopenhauer's pessimistic view of the unconscious, and his pessimism about sexualized and intimate love, is at odds with the view that a life can go well in ordinary and undramatic ways. For this reason it may jar with our own experience. A defender of Schopenhauer might point to the impressively large ranks of those who have been disappointed in love, but those who are more optimistic may still point to the, perhaps thinner, ranks of those who have loved and who seem to have lived well because of it. All of us may at least hope to be unlike Schopenhauer, and to find ourselves among the lucky few.

The background to love

A more troubling form of pessimism about love, and again a pessimism that especially targets sexualized love, can be rooted in a quite different background story about the past, a story that focuses on the personal history of the individual rather than the history of the species. As unique, particular beings we are all formed and shaped by our past. By appeal to this consideration, Freud and Proust tell us that love is blind (or at least partially sighted) and that our attitude towards those we claim to love is shaped by a personal history in which our loved one will have played little or no role.

Freud sets out this position in his seminal 1914 paper "On Narcissism" via the claim that love is generally of two kinds. First (and particularly in the case of women and homosexuals) there is *narcissistic* love: we love ourselves not only in our present form, but in past and future forms as well and we love our children because they were once a part of us. We may also love a religious ideal of perfection because it is related to an envisaged future self with all faults purged away. The second kind of love (which is more common among men) is *anaclitic* love, a form of attachment in which we attempt to relive the past. There is, for example, the love of young men for sexual partners who bear a curious resemblance to younger versions of their own mothers. But love's delusions need not be so straightforward. Freud is nuanced in ways that take his pessimism beyond that of Schopenhauer. The attempt to relive the past can assume many a subtle guise. In the *Three Essays on the Theory of Sexuality* (1905) Freud had already pointed out that:

> A child's affection for his parents is no doubt the most impor-tant infantile trace which, after being revived at puberty, points the way to his choice of an object; but it is not the only one. Other starting-points with the same early origin enable a man to develop more than one *sexual line*, based no less upon his childhood, and to lay down various conditions for his object-choice. (1984: 152)

These types of love, the *narcissistic* and the *anaclitic*, may seem very different, but Freud is clear that they both emerge out of the individual's history and especially the individual's early history. Insight into the past turns out to be insight into the unconscious with each of us bringing something like a model or prototype to our adult relationships. It is then tempting to say that in some sense our love always remains *about* the model or prototype.

The finer details of Freud's account may, of course, be challenged. The gendered distinction that makes women largely narcissistic looks suspiciously like the rationalization of a prejudice, although the suggestion that men are, at the deepest level of their being, infantile, may seem slightly closer to the truth. There is, at least, no continuation of Schopenhauer's openly declared war against women, although there are suggestions elsewhere in Freud that women are particularly deficient, lacking and envious of male completeness. Even so, Freud's central claim is hard to dismiss: to some extent we love *because* of our past. This may place a question mark over the genuineness of our love for a spouse or partner. After all, we may want to be with them now but they formed no part of that all-too-decisive past. The same may also be said about the love that others may claim to have for us. We may be wrong about being loved or wrong about being loved as we would wish. Freud also recognizes that there is no need to appeal, as Schopenhauer did, to the duplicity and the guile of others. The formation of sexualized love simply takes place in such a way that each of us is caught up in our own egocentric drama and this allows love more than enough scope to lead us into folly.

Proust tells a story that has important similarities, although his apparent concern with the opposite sex is, at times, paper thin. Proust's cycle of slowly paced novels, *A Remembrance of Things Past* (1913–27), begins with a narrator who recalls a childhood longing for his mother, a longing that she should comfort him at night and his distress when she repeatedly refused to do so. This childish longing lingers on and on. It feeds into the nocturnal restlessness that the narrator suffers from during his adult years. Turning in early, he would often fall asleep and wake up at night-time: "I would be astonished to find myself in a state of darkness, pleasant and restful enough for my eyes, but even more, perhaps, for my mind, to which it appeared incomprehensible, without a cause, something dark indeed" (2002: 1). As the novels unfold we see how the past has shaped the present capacity for love, with characters able to fully recognize and to acknowledge love only in the absence of their loved one or only when it is too late, when love has failed. Proust regards love for art as a safer bet than love for humans, a trick that Schopenhauer would have admired but that Freud views as narcissistic. Like Freud, Proust acknowledges the pointlessness and folly of attempting to avoid sexualized intimate love. We cannot help longing for that which is never quite available.

In their different ways, Freud and Proust place stress on the shaping of love by that which is absent or lost in time. For both, our loving appreciation of another is always shot through with personal-historic influences from our formation as needy, erotic beings who long for love and for the presence of another. But in so far as the others we love have to fit in with some pre-established pattern, we may begin to wonder about the sense in which our love is really about them and the sense in which their love can really be about us. This is a context in which pessimism about the nature of love can flourish and spill over into a personal scepticism about being loved as we would wish to be loved or, more simply, loved for who we truly are.

It may be tempting to respond to such doubts by claiming that everyone is entitled to a past and that it is unwise for any of us to pry too closely into the mechanisms and history of another's soul. Alternatively, it may be tempting to engage in a philosophical sleight-of-hand by distinguishing in an unbridgeably strict manner between the true *object* of someone's love and the *causes* of their love. Admittedly, a more rough-and-ready distinction of this sort can often make sense. Any of us may relate it to our own lives. In my own case, I love Suzanne *partly* because of events that took place before we met, events in which she played no part. That is to say, I accept that these events have helped to bring about my love and that without them I might never have come to feel the way I do. But there is an important sense in which my love is still *about* Suzanne. She may still be the object of my love even if she is not its sole cause. In recognition of this, I may say something of the following sort: "My past prepared me to love Suzanne in a way that it did not prepare me to love others", and this is, no doubt, true. Similarly, her love for me can genuinely be a love *for me* although it is partly the result of events in which I played no role, events that I am unaware of or aware of only faintly, events that she will tell me about if and when she is ready to do so, or perhaps never. And that's fine too.

But there are times when a rigid separation of love's *objects* and its historic *causes* does not seem quite right. After all, some emotions can be the genuine item only if they arise out of the right kind of sequence of events. Grief is one example. We cannot truly grieve for someone we do not know; we cannot experience grief that is genuinely *about* them if we have not, in the past, cared for them. Anything else, such as the excitement experienced by those who just happen to be caught up in a wave of popular mourning, involves a grief that is false, a response that is other than it seems. Moreover, it is not unreasonable to point out that each new grief recapitulates some or all of those that have gone before. When we mourn, we awaken old feelings of loss that have lain dormant but have never quite gone away. There is more than one sense in which real grief is partly *about* the present and partly *about* the past.

One way to generalize here is to say that grief has a mixed intentionality, that is, a mixed *aboutness*. And, among the emotions, this is a normal circumstance. Consider anger. A man becomes angry with his misbehaving children after a particularly frustrating day at work. Because of the background to the emotion we may be inclined to say that the anger is not exclusively or even primarily about them or about their current actions. It may be, to some extent, about these actions but also about what went before. And in view of this, the anger may seem excessive or simply inappropriate.

So why should we not think of love in the same way as partly a response to the present and also, in part, a response to the past? Faced with the idea that love is not exclusively a response to an immediately present loved one, we may retreat behind the defence that love is an exception and that what applies in the case of other emotions does not apply here. Up to a point this is no doubt true. Love is, in various respects, anomalous. It is not, for example, episodic in the narrowest sense. Emotions such as anger, joy and fear may briefly occur. It makes sense to say that I was afraid or joyful for fifteen minutes on Wednesday afternoon but it makes no sense to say that I was in love with someone on Tuesday for a similar length of time, shortly before lunch but not afterwards. Love is different from other emotions in this and other respects. But whatever it is that makes love different does not obviously prevent it from having mixed intentionality and being, in some respects, about the past as well as the present.

Such mixed intentionality, and the influence of the past on the formation and character of love, is something we may be aware of even in the absence of familiarity with any complex Freudian or Proustian background theory. Worries concerning such matters may be just as familiar from old black-and-white films. Let us set the scene. The tastefully dressed new lady of the house has married her husband after a whirlwind romance and returns home to the ancestral hall only to find a painting there of her husband's first wife, an expensively dressed and imposing woman who died in tragic circumstances but who is strikingly similar in appearance to his new wife. Just who does this man love? Well, partly his love seems to be for person X and partly it seems to be for person Y who is now dead. But which one does he love more? Dramatic and melodramatic examples may help us to recognize that the past will influence who any of us are capable of loving and the way in which we are capable of loving them. As a result, things can sometimes go badly wrong. An earlier love or attachment may continue to haunt a present relationship in obvious and telling ways.

In contrast to the above scenario, the other person's past may remain a largely hidden country and this can lead to sceptical doubts about being loved or to doubts about being loved in the right way and to the exclusion of all others. Such uncertainty may be more plausible than the specialized Schopenhauerian fear that life, nature, biology and the unconscious have conspired to trick us into loving someone, or to trick someone into loving us, when we are merely good breeding stock. In my own case, I am in moderately good condition but accept that, apart from my wits, I have very few biological lures. Suzanne could easily trade-up for a better model if she wanted to. But she does not do so and does not want to do so. I do not worry that a need to find good breeding stock has impelled her towards sharing a life with me. When I look around,

I also find that the oddest people have ended up with each other, and not merely as a matter of default. But the past is another matter and, from time to time, it can give any of us a greater cause for concern. After all, we want to be loved and we do not want to be just a convenient safe haven. We also want to be loved for who we are and not simply for our similarities to someone else or because we are vaguely reminiscent of a childhood ideal. We do not want to be an unsuspecting outlet for long pent-up feelings that we did not help to induce.

Nonetheless, even a recognition of the mixed intentionality of love, a recognition of the fact that it is always, *in some sense*, about more than an immediately present human, does not set up a compelling case for either pessimism about the nature of love or for scepticism about being loved. We may, instead, hold to the view that "Love involves seeing someone as unique and special but doing so in the light of what we know of their past and also in the light of our own past". And this is not at all the same as claiming that "Love is always primarily a response to the past and only takes the guise of a response to the present".

Instead, to bring matters into focus by appeal to a personal and autobiographical case, I want to say that Suzanne sees me in the light of her past, and that I see her in the light of mine. In this untroubling sense our love is not *simply* about the immediately present other. Our apparently immediate loving relation is always mediated by our personal histories and by our shared life together. We may both see more clearly as a result. After all, it is only against the background of the past that any of us can recognize genuine kindness and a good heart. But here I speak of an *entire* past without according an overall privilege to infancy in the manner of Freud and Proust (or even in the manner of post-Freudians such as Bowlby). Infancy may occupy a special place, but once we begin to legislate in favour of the unvarying primacy of the infantile there will be little hope for any of us.

In so far as someone's past helps to make them who they are, we should also want it to influence the way in which they see us. The result will then be a way of seeing that is informed by the complex and historically shaped fibre of their being and does not emerge out of any momentary and charming whim. Sometimes the past that influences their way of seeing will involve us and sometimes it will not. The former can be particularly reassuring but the latter need not disturb. When I realize, as from time to time I do, that Suzanne is kinder than anyone else I have ever known, I am (in part) seeing her in the light of a past that is not her own, but I am seeing her as she really is, in an utterly realistic way. But I am also (in part) seeing her in the light of our shared history. In the same way, any two individuals who accumulate years together will become a crucial part of each other's history. In my own case, I have lived with Suzanne for eighteen years now and we have known each other since the end of our teens. We are not old but we are no longer young and our time together accounts for a considerable portion of our lives. If one of us should ask, "Is your love really about me?", it would make sense for the other to say, "Well, who else would it be about?" Unless we are determined to privilege childhood experience over the greater bulk of our history, there will be no good reason to regard this response as unsatisfactory even though there is a great deal that it does not say. If we want to understand as much as we can about love, and about the concept of love, it is not a conversation stopper.

3. The depth of love

It is a striking circumstance that most of the great pessimists about love have refused to dismiss it as a trivial matter, as a temporary perturbation of our wits that might easily be avoided. One fictional exception to this norm is the character Benedick in Shakespeare's *Much Ado About Nothing*. Benedick mocks the romantic adventures of his friends and protests that he will never lose more blood with love than he can get again with drinking. But even among pessimists Benedick remains something of an anomaly. And, in the course of time, he is stricken down with love in such a way that the naive quality of his earlier folly is thrown into sharp relief. The love that he cannot ultimately deny serves as a reminder that we may influence and shape our love but *loving* or *not loving* is beyond our deliberate, moment-to-moment control. There are things that we can do to try to fall out of love and things that we can do to fall into it. We can prepare the ground or put barriers in its way, and this is one of the reasons why we can be praised or blamed for loving someone. But love itself is not chosen.

In general, pessimists about the nature of love are aware of the limits of our control and try to prepare us against love's inevitable onset. By doing so they acknowledge the depth of our urge to love and the difficult-to-handle place it occupies within our lives. But love is a force that can overwhelm us even when it is anticipated. To speak here of what is deep and to deploy the metaphor of depth is an obvious way to put matters. However it is not altogether clear what love's depth involves. More is at stake than the obvious claim that love can be intense or intensely felt, although this is also true. Intensity and depth are not the same thing. Perhaps an element of obscurity is implied when we say that love is deep rather than shallow, the suggestion being that we cannot see all the way down to the bottom of the pool, that something remains hidden, something eludes us. The father of existentialism, Søren Kierkegaard, writes about love's depth in just this way:

> From whence comes love, where does it have its origin and its source; where is the place, its stronghold, from which it proceeds? Certainly this place is hidden or is in that which is hidden. There is a place in a human being's most inward depths; from this place proceeds the life of love.   (2009: 26)

On this view, love is deep because it is bound up with our humanity and more specifically with a "need" to love: "For him in whom there is love to his neighbour, love is a need, the deepest need. He does not have need of men just to have someone to love, but he needs to love men" (2009: 78).

The love that Kierkegaard concerns himself with in this latter instance is the love of neighbours that is required by the Bible, a love that he takes to be every bit as real as love that is both sexualized and intimate. In some respects he regards neighbour love as more admirable and profound but he refuses to see these loves as utterly separate phenomena. What joins them together, at least in *Works of Love* (1847) but not always in his later writings, is a longing or "need" to reach out beyond the human and to embrace the divine. For Kierkegaard, this is what we are doing when we love neighbours and this is what we are doing when we love our spouse in a more intimate and sexualized manner. On this view, the love of two people for each other *always* points towards a centre of love beyond them both and this centre of love is God.

This is not a novel claim. Plato also held that love teaches us to look towards something transcendent and that a connection to, or a figurative *memory of*, the latter is what we shall find when we search our innermost depths for an understanding of love. A slight nuance here is that Kierkegaard writes about our need to love while Plato writes about love in a way that makes it part of our humanity rather than a special kind of compulsion. But both make the connection between love and the desire for proximity to the transcendent and what is involved is not so much a desire to seize hold of and to possess, but a desire to be with and to be in the presence of the divine, a desire that the divine should touch our lives.

Such a view is unlikely to impress anyone who regards their outlook on life as thoroughly modern and, by virtue of being modern, *not* religious. But here we should remember that there is a gulf between claiming that humans have a deep longing for something more than human and the quite different claim that there is actually is a *transcendent something* or a God who might answer and respond to such a longing. The belief that human love reaches out beyond all that is human, or that we have a deep need to love, a need that arises out of our incompleteness and lack of self-sufficiency, does not automatically shift us away from moral psychology and into theology.

However, it also does not place love beyond the bounds of pessimism and doubt. The fact that we may need to love, or that we love because it is part of our nature to do so, does not require that we love in a lucid and clear-sighted manner. But once we have a firm hold on the idea that love leads us to look beyond the self, it may then be tempting to regard it as a bulwark against the kind of egocentricity that generates fantasy and delusion. The temptation will then be to regard love and insight as closely related. And this too can be regarded as a way in which love may be something deep. It is, after all, counter-intuitive to associate depth (of whatever sort) with sheer fantasy. And this may be a problem for any pessimist about the nature of love who wants to hold on to the idea that love truly is something that arises out of our depths. By contrast, those who *reject* pessimism about the nature of love are able to say that love is deep because it is *not* based on delusions of any sort and fantasy least of all. A contrast with both the obvious and with the merely delusional may be in play whenever we say that love is deep or profound.

But to say this is not quite the same as claiming that "Depth implies truth". There are, after all, beliefs and imaginative narratives that are deep but not straightforwardly true. Religion and literature can both be deep but to say this is not to suggest that the associated narratives are an accurate retelling of events. What is at stake in the claim that both can be deep is the important idea that they are not always mere fantasy *because*, although not literally true, they nonetheless draw our attention to something real and important. Often what they draw our attention to is an overlooked or neglected feature of human life.

A great deal can be said about how we may best separate out *that which is fantasy* from *that which is imaginative* and about how to prevent this distinction from hardening into an absolute dichotomy. But in relation to the concept of depth we may still say something simple: we may still say that what is deep cannot involve a wholesale flight from the real; it cannot *simply* be escapist or delusional in any sense that would reduce to fantasy. While this makes it awkward for pessimists about the nature of love to accommodate the idea that love is *both* delusional and deep, it may not be altogether impossible for them to do so. Schopenhauer suggests that, although delusional, love is nonetheless important because it is connected to and shapes familiar human desires and experiences. It is delusional but it is not sheer fantasy. In a sense it does direct our attention to what is real, specifically to biologically suitable mating partners, but it also generates a systematically false view of their merits, a view that simultaneously deceives and motivates us to act. But what it motivates us to do is not in our own best interests. In a sense, we are entangled in love, as in a web, and cannot escape from it because it extends all the way through our being.

On this view, the lure of love or the temptation to love is not something we can avoid or choose to forego. Experiencing love's temptations is part of what it is to be human even if true wisdom demands that we then try to resist them. The presupposition here is that love is too deep a part of being human for us to escape, but an ongoing path of renunciation may still be available. From this point of view, where Shakespeare's Benedick went wrong was not in his suspicion about love as a trickster and a deceiver, but in his extremely foolish underestimation of its wiles, depth and resourcefulness. Benedick chose to regard love as something shallow, as mere fantasy. A more intelligent and plausible pessimism about love holds that there is more to it: that loving or a need to love is also a deep part of who and what we are. For the Schopenhauerian pessimist, because of love's depth, unless we are constantly on our guard, it will lure us off to places where we should not go.

This is pessimism in the truest sense: not simply a light-hearted suspicion about love but the view that love appears to enrich our lives while covertly damaging and subverting any chance that we may have of personal independence and peace of mind. For a pessimist of this stamp, love is delusional in a special sense that binds it to our equally delusional pursuit of happiness, to our efforts to live as well as possible and to what Schopenhauer regards as our exaggerated sense of the possibilities of doing so. This is pessimism about love that is embedded in a larger pessimism about human life in general. But here we may ask "Are life and love really like this?" It is not obvious that both must always go quite so badly.

Embracing love

Schopenhauer's contemporary, the novelist Stendhal, embraced pessimism about the nature of love in a far more light-hearted manner, without any resentful hostility. Unlike Schopenhauer, he was an enthusiastic player in what he took to be love's deceptive game. But, like Schopenhauer, he was also notably unsuccessful in love. Stendhal's track record is a counterpoint to that of Julien Sorel, the central character in his novel *Scarlet and Black* (1830). The youthful and apparently resourceful Sorel, plagued by a fashion-able inner anguish and by a sense of rejection, causes mayhem by seducing a series of women who ultimately do not resist his charms, although on occasion he succeeds only because they take pity on a confused young man. By contrast with Sorel, Stendhal's own love-life veered towards the prosaically unsuccessful. For several years he pursued and tried to win the affections of the Italian political activist Mathilde Dembowski, who seems to have been bemused, at times annoyed and occasionally inconvenienced by his attentions.

In the latter stages of this fruitless quest, Stendhal wrote a cele-brated study, *On Love* (1822), an extended treatment of the emotion. In its pages he allows that there is something fundamentally foolish about love and especially about falling in love. He allows that there is a sense in which it does involve motivation by delusion. But for Stendhal, it is motivation by delusion of an imaginative and some-times delightful sort; it directs our attention and our actions in life-enhancing ways. Love may make fools of us all but it is in our interests to become love's fools. Doing so is intimately connected to the *genuine* possibility of well-being. Love lifts us out of the commonplace and the mundane by allowing the appearance of admirable properties to "crystallize" on the ordinary and the dull.

> Leave a lover with his thoughts for twenty-four hours, and
> this is what will happen: At the salt mines of Salzburg, they

> throw a leafless wintery bough into one of the abandoned workings. Two or three months later they haul it out covered with a shining deposit of crystals … The original branch is no longer recognisable. What I have called crystallization is a mental process which draws from everything that happens new proofs of the perfection of the loved one.   (1975: 45)

On this account, love is still delusional but again it is not sheer fantasy. Love's temptation and lure is only there for those who connect with the world in a special way. It is only there for those who have the imagination to see something more than the boring and the commonplace. It is the price we pay for having a lively and, above all, healthy attitude towards the rest of the world. It is the price of living to the utmost and as well as we can.

This suggests a different sense in which love may be understood as deep and, by being deep, important. According to Stendhal, love is not deep because it is biologically or naturally embedded in our being in a way that makes the temptations of love unavoidable. The unimaginative *can* avoid them, but those with imagination and spirit will not want to do so. Love is a welcome ally in the constant struggle against boredom and pointlessness; it is deep because it is bound up not simply with being human, but with human flourishing, with a genuinely available well-being, even if it is a well-being that is pursued by many but secured only by the happy few.

Working in different ways with these themes of love's connection to our desire to live well, and its pervasive influence on who we are and how we act, Schopenhauer and Stendhal both recognized the importance of love and the special importance of sexualized intimate love. But influential pessimists about the nature of love, Freud and Proust in particular, have tended to agree with Schopenhauer, Plato and Kierkegaard about the urge to love being inbuilt while they have also tended to agree with Stendhal, Plato and (arguably) Kierkegaard that any attempt systematically to resist the urge to love *is* folly, repressive and perhaps even pathological. We may sensibly resist the urge to love this or that person, and we may at least try to be discriminating about who we love at any given time, but we cannot sensibly resist sexualized intimate love in a wholesale manner. To do so is to reject what we are and to reject any possibility of living well.

The contemporary philosopher Mary Midgley captures this same point about the indispensability of love by appeal to a thought experiment. She invites us to imagine that an offer has been made in good faith and by well-trusted, intelligent and reliable beings from another planet. These obliging aliens propose to adopt some of our surplus and vulnerable infants and to rear them under apparently favourable conditions, without the hunger, disease, abuse and misery that a good number of them might otherwise suffer. According to Midgley, what *could* lead us to reject this offer, or at least to consider doing so in some cases, would be the answer of such aliens to questions about their emotional life and practices, questions such as "What meaning do they attach to such words as love?" (1983: 107). The aliens' lack of any equivalent to our key emotional concepts, and in particular their lack of any concept of love, could give us a good reason to believe that, in spite of fine and noble intentions, the infants would not be raised in a sufficiently human way. Lacking a concept of love, the alien and non-human beings would also lack an appreciation of love's indispensable role in human flourishing or, more simply, its role in a human life that is well-lived.

Perhaps Midgley's position shows insufficient regard for the terrible and obscene nature of human poverty. After all, who but someone who was well fed would have qualms about a convenient poverty-eliminating arrangement? And perhaps, *more persuasively*, it may be objected that in the light of such a generous offer these non-humans simply *must* have a concept of love, albeit one we do not quite understand. Nonetheless, if we happen to *believe* that they have no concept of love there will be a dilemma. Although material well-being is necessary to any kind of good life, love may also be indispensable to such a life, albeit in a different way.

However, there are some risks involved in connecting love and well-being, especially if the connection is understood in an overly simplistic manner. It is far from obvious that "Love is all you need" or that "Love conquers all" (claims made respectively by the Beatles and the poet Virgil). It isn't and it doesn't. A similarly overstated account of love is involved in the view that "In the end, all our failures are failures of love". This comment, put into the mouth of a character in an Iris Murdoch novel, accurately reflects Dante's assessment of love's standing in his *Divine Comedy* (1308–21), where all failings turn out to involve insufficient love or excessive love or love that is misdirected. Such claims may sound impressive and deep, but treating love as all important can carry great risks. It places heavy demands on love and, understood primarily in the context of a love that is sexualized and intimate, it places *too many* demands on the person who is loved.

Plato warns us about the dangers of understanding love in this way in the *Symposium*. He warns us by means of an impressive myth that is placed in the mouth of the inebriated playwright Aristophanes, one of the central characters of the dialogue. It is a fiction, but nonetheless a fiction that directs our attention to something real: in the beginning we were all complete, happy and highly mobile. Each one of us had four arms and four legs and we could rotate all the way around and roll along, at speed, from one place to another. We were such wonderful creatures that we felt ourselves a rival to the gods. And so, to teach us a lesson, to show their power and to put us in our place, the gods took a decision to split us down the middle, leaving each part with two arms and two legs and gathering all the spare flesh together at the navel. Even to this day, as soon as we believe that we have found our other half we rush headlong towards them. Ignoring all sorts of obstacles, we try desperately to become entangled. We try to become whole again (Plato, *Symposium* 189d–194e).

The imagery is striking. It connects well with the experience of what it is like to love, that is, with the phenomenology of sexualized love, and especially with the experience of falling in love. Doing so involves passion, rushing headlong; in part it is a matter of desire but it can also be like the healing of an old wound; we may feel that we have known the other person all our lives, even if we have only known them for a short period of time; the person we love seems to *complete* us or at least to offer the possibility of a rounded completeness. There are aspects of this complex and beautiful image that Plato wants to retain and other aspects about which he is uneasy. Love may be deep in the sense that a life without love would be less than a fully human life, but the idea that the other person will complete us threatens to place an unbearable strain and burden on love and on the person we love, a person who, in obvious respects, will always retain their separateness. It is excessively demanding to require that they alone, and without regard to circumstance, should make us happy and whole. After all, the well-being or happiness of any human is liable to require something more and other than intimate love, or love of any sort.

To say this is not to deny that love is a major and indispensable part of what we need if life is to go well, but it is difficult to see how love, or loving and being loved, could be anything other than one major requirement among others. Love cannot heal all wounds, overcome all obstacles and make the wounded whole. Those who have been damaged by life, or subjected to some dreadful physical trauma, may need urgently to be loved, but they may also and more urgently need medical attention. Chance misfortune, illness and the structural malevolence of social and political institutions may still get in our way no matter what we, or those we love, happen to do. And when, in the face of such obstacles, a life happens to go badly, we need not assume that the misfortune results from our having loved the wrong person or from their failure to render what is due. To say this is simply to accept that a life can fail in all sorts of interesting and mundane ways that have nothing at all to do with a failure of love or with the shortcomings of a partner or spouse. Accepting this is not at all the same thing as failing to recognize love's importance, its depth or the fact that, for humans, it is required for well-being. Love can still be an indispensable part of a good life. It can still be something we need even though it is not all we need.

Why is love indispensable to a good life?

Love of any sort involves seeing someone as special, and doing so in the light of our own past and in the light of what we know about their past. But it is not only about *seeing favourably* or about holding a particular set of favourable beliefs. It is also, as Plato realized, about *wanting, desiring* and even *needing*. It has an erotic dimension in the sense that it involves a directly sexual component or else it can be understood by analogy with sex or by analogy with sexual desire. But whether or not the *seeing, believing* and *desiring* that love involves are discrete and separable mental states is a point on which I shall remain officially neutral, although at times I am tempted to say that they are more closely bound together.

The fact that loving is, in part, about *desiring* is particularly obvious in the case of sexualized love. When we love someone in this sense we *want* to be with them and we *want* them to be happy. We also *want* to be loved in return. But *loving* and *being loved* can be regarded as something deeper than desire. It can, as Kierkegaard suggested in the case of *loving*, be seen as a basic human *need*. In favouring this approach I realize that I may be opening myself up to a charge of sentimentality. It is all very well to say pleasant things about love, to say that it is, in some difficult-to-specify way, deep and necessary to a good life, but any one of us may be inclined to ask "Well, is it really?" After all, there seems to be nothing very wrong with the idea that someone could live out their life with self-respect while moving through a succession of mutually enjoyable relationships without ever feeling a strong desire or any *need* for something more intimate. Such a life might simply involve seeing others as they really are, without the elaborate ornamentation of love. Claims about a basic human need for love, and especially about a need *to be loved*, may then seem dangerously close to a justification for the neurotic, for the insecure and for those who are psychologically "needy". Perhaps humans who were fully at ease with themselves would have no such requirement. We may even suspect, as so many futuristic writers have done, that an efficient and functional world would dispense with love just as it might dispense with the inefficient privatized rearing of infants. Aldous Huxley's *Brave New World* explores this possibility, as does *Logan's Run* by William F. Nolan and George Clayton Johnson.

We do, however, have good reasons to hope that such a situation will never come to pass, and to trust that humans will continue to appreciate love's importance. What follows, although far from a complete account of why love matters, will try to offer clues, and will draw attention to two of the main reasons why love, especially sexualized love, is so important to a life that is well lived. But these are reasons of quite different sorts. The first is consistent with pessimism about the nature of love while the second is in tension with it. The first is Stendhal's point, which is also Plato's point and Schopenhauer's fear: that love helps to motivate us and to give our lives shape and direction. We may often fail to notice it, but the places where we live, the jobs we do and the way we spend our time are all influenced by a concern for those we love. When we love someone, especially in a sexualized manner, we want to secure their love and we want our happiness and their happiness to result from our doing so, even though we may sometimes, or often, be confused about how this much-desired outcome is to be achieved. In the absence of love, if there was nothing and no one that we cared for, we would be frequently directionless and habitually bored.

Harry G. Frankfurt, using a philosophical vocabulary that was unavailable to either Stendhal or Schopenhauer, has defended love's indispensability on this same basis, as a means to fend off a lack of direction:

> Love is the originating source of terminal value. If we loved nothing, then nothing would possess for us any definitive and inherent worth. There would be nothing that we found ourselves in any way constrained to accept as a final end. By its very nature, loving entails both that we regard its objects as valuable in themselves and that we have no choice but to adopt those objects as our final ends.　　　(2004: 55–6)

Stendhal and Frankfurt agree on love's positive motivational role, even though they differ in their preferred exemplars of love. Stendhal favours the more romantic early stages of sexualized intimate love while Frankfurt favours a special kind of self-love, a self-love that is shorn of any disreputable selfishness or egocentricity.

Against either view, we might hold that there are different but just as motivationally effective ways of getting things done. We may imagine the possibility of care that does not involve love, the possibility of being motivated by an emotion of some other sort. But while this prospect appears promising from a distance, looked at more closely it is less attractive. Motivation by sympathy is one possible alternative, but sympathy on the part of those who lack any love may seem too much like the emotion of an unengaged spectator, and too weak an influence to guide our day-to-day lives. Alternatively there is pity and there is compassion. And while we might wonder about compassion, it does at least make sense to say that we can pity those we do not love. We might pity others, or ourselves, and this could motivate us to refrain from all sorts of harms and to engage in all sorts of positive actions. Pity has often been associated with the active life especially when it is the life of some healthy, robust or simply dominant being who is faced with the defeated and the less fortunate.

To bolster the case for pity as a fundamental source of motivation, it may be pointed out that a failure to show pity under some circumstances can be a real and obvious moral failure. At the close of Virgil's *Aeneid* (19 BCE), the epic Roman poem that takes as its theme the founding of the city in the face of opposition from the natives, Aeneas stands over the last of his enemies and faces a moment of decision. Should he spare the life of a defeated adversary or mercilessly, and without pity, slay him? The decision is both personal and political: an allegory for Roman character and power. The enemy is utterly crushed, no longer and never again to be a threat. These circumstances are set up, contrived, to allow Aeneas to show pity for a defeated enemy, just as Achilles and the Greek heroes had shown pity at some of their finest and most human moments. He could accept that there must be a limit to suffering and to revenge and that Rome must be more than powerful. Instead, Aeneas sees that his enemy is wearing a trophy, the buckler of a slain friend. Rage seizes him and in his anger, single-mindedly and without pity, he exacts his bloody revenge. The poem ends.

The example is intended to illustrate a simple point: *failure* to show pity is a real event. But precisely because pity is so bound up with a perceived inequality, it is a suspect motive. Even self-pity involves feeling that we have fallen *below* a norm of well-being, so, in an important sense, inequality is still an issue. Sometimes, and perhaps often, pity can involve a covert form of contempt; it can function as an outlet for what Nietzsche called "ressentiment". In this respect, pity can be a source of motivation that lacks the vitality of the more tonic emotions.

Love, because it involves valuing in a positive sense, seems to be unusually or uniquely effective at motivating our actions and, at least sometimes, uniquely effective at motivating us to act in a genuinely caring and life-affirming manner. A person may carry on, from day to day, without any special purpose and then be surprised by love. The *wanting* and *longing* of love may bring them more fully back to life. Given the pervasiveness of love, the way it works its way unseen into so much of what we do, and the way it provides a major reason why we do it, there may be a difficulty in specifying any other emotion or any combination of emotions that could play exactly the same role. Should any cluster of emotions manage to do so, we might suspect that they must involve love of some sort. Compassion that is quite different from pity may give rise to the same suspicion. When Schopenhauer advocates compassion in his later writings, as a general guide to our relations with others, he significantly constrains his pessimism about love. He shows that he is not a pessimist about every kind of love but only about sexualized intimate love as opposed to the love of our neighbour. Even so, this move is still guided by a broader pessimism about the possibility of well-being in a world where compassion is universally called for.

Although I want to say that love is supremely effective at what it does, this alone would not make it indispensable. It may be good and desirable that love is part of our lives, but it may still be an exaggeration to say that it is deep in the sense of being something we *need*. And even if we accept that love of some sort happens to be indispensable to a well-motivated life, there remains something vaguely unsatisfactory about the idea that love's importance or depth reduces to this motivational effectiveness. There is, surely, *more* to the depth and importance of love, more to our *need* for love, than its ability to keep us busy and oriented towards our daily tasks. Any explanation of love's importance that relied solely on such a role might risk turning the object of our affections, the person or persons we happen to love, into little more than a convenient but arbitrary focus for the work of life's great organizing force. This danger can perhaps be seen in Stendhal. His love turns out to be a very one-sided drama.

A robust extension of the claim that love is *necessary* to a good life, for reasons that are related to motivation, involves the claim that love leads us to look outwards and truthfully beyond ourselves. Plato, Thomas Aquinas, Dante and, in more recent years, Iris Murdoch, have all claimed that love for others (and especially for a particular other person) is an indispensable component of our moral education because it teaches us the extremely difficult lesson that someone else is real. As such, it is a step towards the realization that we are a small, if important, part of a larger reality that exceeds us and that is, in various and obvious ways, more important than any of us. And even if love is able to challenge our egocentricity only *to some extent* it still helps to motivate us *to some extent* in the right way, in a way that allows a partial release from the self-punitive drama of egocentric preoccupation. If this view is right then hell is not other people. It is, rather, a failure of openness, a failure of love and a consequent and dreadful entrapment within the self. It is no accident that Milton speaks of a "hell within" in the section of *Paradise Lost* (1667) where his dynamic but misguided and rebellious Satan turns away from mankind in sadness while accepting that these are creatures of another mould "whom my thoughts pursue with wonder, and could love". Love of others and his hell within are mutually exclusive (2004: bk 4, lines 62–3). It is also no accident that Dante also represents hell as an enclosed space: a bell-like interior that contrasts with the mountainous but redemptive path of his Purgatory, where love redeems and is redeemed and where movement may be restricted but still occurs in an open space, exposed to all that is outside.

I am almost entirely in sympathy with this ego-breaking view of love: the view that love alone can save us from ourselves. While egocentricity may lay all manner of traps for us, the love of others may ensure that it does not have matters all its own way. Nonetheless, the plausibility of this view will depend on the claim that love for others, or apparent love for others, is not another cunning drama put together by the self. That is to say, it will depend on a decisive rejection of pessimism about the nature of love and in particular a decisive rejection of pessimism about the life-shaping experience of sexualized intimate love. Rather than associating love with delusion, this approach associates love with a clarity of vision that feeds into well-motivated action but that is also to be prized in its own right. Given this requirement for a robust rejection of pessimism about the nature of love, it is an approach that will be more plausible in the light of all that follows. But it will not be presupposed. What follows may also help to ensure that this approach can be formulated in a sufficiently cautious and lucid manner without any oversimplification of the complex relation between love for others and concern for oneself.

Quite apart from love's motivational role, there is a second dimension to love's indispensability. Love is indispensable to human well-being because of our need *to be loved*, although the determined pessimist about the nature of love may regard such a need as little more than neurotic. What I want to suggest, instead, is that the experience of being loved, the belief or the awareness or the knowledge that we are or have been loved, is crucial to our sense of value or worth. When we are loved we are able to see ourselves in a new and better light. But we can do so only if we are open to an acceptance of the love in question and are not entrapped in any ongoing scepticism about being loved. Seeing ourselves in such a light also requires that we see the love in question as an authoritative response and not as fundamentally delusional. That is to say, our contentment and sense of worth requires us to overcome any wholesale form of pessimism about the nature of love and to remain open to the possibility of being loved in a *realistic* and *truthful* manner.

Such openness to love can be a difficult virtue to sustain, but it is a key human virtue because the love that others have for us shows us, in a way that nothing else can, that we matter. This applies to all sorts of love: the love of parents or children, the love of our friends and relations, and even the love that is shown by a devoted pet or companion animal. The latter in particular arouses a special kind of scepticism about love's genuineness but it is not unusual for someone who has suffered extreme personal difficulties to begin to recover a sense of their own worth through the undemanding and unquestioning affection that is given by another creature. Even so, I will suggest that it is the intimate and sexualized love of a partner or spouse that is the most effective way in which we are shown our own value and worth.

When we believe that someone is in love with us we may say, "This person, who could have settled upon any number of others, many of whom have a great deal more going for them, happens to love me. They have a single life to lead and they want to spend it with me rather than anyone else." But even this way of making the point may be unsatisfactory and more than a little self-centred. Knowing or believing that we are loved is not a special kind of personal flattery. It is not, except in superficial respects, akin to coming first in a popularity contest where we assume that the basis for judgement is shallow and the final outcome requires no commitment on the part of those who cast their votes. Instead, the love of a life-partner, spouse or intimate lover involves their desire and often their readiness to share their life with us. It is, perhaps, better to say, "They have a single life to lead and they want us to spend it together".

It may also be misleading to speak about someone "choosing us over all others", given that none of us exactly chooses whom we love. The love that someone has for us is based on the way in which they see us in the light of their own history and in the light of what they know about *our* history. Such a way of seeing runs deeper than mere choice. The love that someone has for us is based on what they want, need and *see in* us. It is not an arbitrary supermarket-style preference for one barely distinguishable product rather than another. Those who love us could, of course, be wildly wrong. They may be deceived even if they are not subject to any special love-inspired delusion. And it may be so surprising that anyone should feel this way about us that we prudently put up a front in order to hold their remarkable misconception in place. But if we are ready to accept that their love is just as genuine as it appears then we may have little option but to recognize that this other person sees us as truly unique and valuable. We may, for the other person, open up all sorts of possibilities of happiness and well-being, but we are not, from their point of view, just a convenient means to secure such ends. Even less are we the apparently suitable breeding stock that Schopenhauer would have us believe. We are regarded, instead, as someone who is *worth* spending a life with.

What may incline us to accept this favourable view as authoritative, rather than delusional, is the reciprocation of love. It is best of all to be loved by someone we love in return. When the person who loves us is no stranger or acquaintance of doubtful insight but is rather someone we love, it gives their affections a standing and authority that they would otherwise lack. There is, after all, little joy to be found in being loved by someone whose judgement is notoriously askew. Similarly, unless we happen to be particularly lonely, few of us would want to have strangers, whose judgement and clarity of vision is untried and untested, turning up at our door and suddenly proclaiming their love.

Appreciation of the role of reciprocation and the authority of the other may help us to recognize that our basic and all-too-human need to be loved is very different from being "needy" in any neurotic sense. We do not need love from just anywhere, even if there is a case for saying that sometimes we ought to be open to the possibility of love from surprising sources. We may not exactly need to be completed by our missing other half, or by the love of one particular person out of all the millions of other humans, but for love to do its work, particularly so in the case of sexualized love, there may need to be some element of trust in the other's judgement and some compatibility of character, a suitable matching and complementing if the love is to have any chance of promoting our happiness and theirs.

When such love is reciprocated, we are loved and regarded as valuable by someone whose own uniqueness and value we are able to appreciate in turn, someone whose views are, on at least some important matters of the heart, regarded as trustworthy and authoritative. But here it may be asked, "Is this really the case?" Perhaps we can imagine loving and being loved by someone who is hopelessly (or charmingly) muddle-headed or who is just a bad judge of character, and our viewing them in this way may cut across any acceptance that their love for us is an indication of our true worth. But such a circumstance is exceptional and comes close to a pastiche of what the familiar experience of reciprocated love is like. This can be better understood when we consider the withdrawal of sexualized love or its loss. It is normal for a great deal of personal turmoil to ensue when we are abandoned by someone who once loved us but who no longer seems to do so. If the relationship has been a long one, we may feel that our world has collapsed or that it has shrunk to smaller dimensions. While similar abandonment feelings are common among the bereaved, they are not based on the deceased having had second thoughts about our merits, about who we are or about our ability to bring joy into their life. When someone leaves us and does not have the good grace to die in order to do so, matters are different. Their departure and the withdrawal of their love can cut us off from an appreciation of our own value under circumstances where our sense of worth has not only been awakened by their love but has also come to be dependent upon its continuity.

Acceptance that their appraisal is, up to a point, authoritative may lead us to say, "Perhaps they were right to leave", or to ask, "Who would want to waste their life on me?" Reflections of this sort can be melodramatic but they may also be an expression of genuine self-doubt; they may indicate a loss of conviction about self-worth. As a protective measure such thoughts may drive us towards pessimism about the nature of love. Rather than face the dangers of loss it may seem better to take the advice of Schopenhauer: to try to limit love's folly, to run from love and, above all, to refuse others the opportunity to make authoritative and all-too-believable judgements about who we are and what we are worth. A genuine openness to love may seem too risky or too much like an invitation to further harm in pursuit of a childish dream that bears little resemblance to a more limited but available and fully adult relationship. By contrast with break-ups and self-doubt, the continuation of a long-term relationship under conditions of love (rather than as a matter of routine) may help to establish and to stabilize a sense of our own value as well as stabilizing our trust in love's genuineness. Under such circumstances, an appreciation that we are *lovable* or *worth loving*, goes hand in hand with an appreciation that we are loved.

To claim, as I have done, that we need to be loved in order to appreciate our own value or worth or, more precisely, to *fully* or *adequately* appreciate our own value or worth, does not mean to say that there is no role in the well-lived life for apartness from others, for solitude, contemplation and silent reflection that periodically removes us from all company or from the company of those we love. It may well be the case that we all need solitude, but not most or all of the time. Similarly, I am not suggesting that we need to be loved (or to believe that we are loved) at each and every moment of our lives. We are not such neurotic creatures that being thrown back on our own resources is always utterly unbearable. What I *am* suggesting is that we need to see ourselves as *lovable* or *worthy of being loved* in order to appreciate our own value, and that such an appreciation of our value or worth is a deep requirement for human contentment. As a claim about moral psychology, as an admittedly value-laden claim that concerns what humans are like, I am suggesting that the only effective way in which this appreciation that we are lovable creatures can be brought about is by the recognition that we are loved or that we have been loved at some previous time, or minimally, by the *belief* that we are or have been loved. Hypothetical scenarios, envisaged by those who are aware that they have never been loved, will not do.

4. A sense of worth

It is difficult to imagine what it would be like to live without the recognition that humans matter. Our preferred terminology ("worth" or "value" or "intrinsic value" or "inherent worth") is secondary to the belief or the recognition that is involved. We can, of course, utter all sorts of impressive statements about morality being a sham and human importance a fiction, but none of us live by such a view. Nor could we live by it. In our commonplace actions, every day and in all sorts of ways, we show that we regard humans as more than obstacles to be navigated and tools to be used. Other and earlier humans have, arguably, held the more restricted view that *some* humans matter, or that *local* humans matter or that one particular group of humans matters, but to be human has always, in some way, involved the belief in, or recognition of, value. We are, in that respect, moral animals. It is part of our make-up.

I have suggested that love discloses this value in a way that nothing else can and that we need to see ourselves as lovable, as worthy of being loved and as potential recipients of love, in order to appreciate our own value. I have placed some emphasis on this rather than on the related idea that nothing discloses the value of *others* in quite the same way that love does. In this respect my approach contrasts with that of the Australian philosopher Raimond Gaita, who states that "Sometimes we see that something is precious only in the light of someone's love for it" (2004: 24). This is a claim I would not want to dispute. It involves an understanding of love's disclosive role that is informed by Gaita's personal experience during his early years as a hospital porter, when he witnessed the love of a nun for the patient she diligently visited, a love that showed Gaita the worth of the patient in a way that the care of doctors did not. He suspects (perhaps rightly) that this love was shaped by the nun's experience of parental love and by the language of love that figured in her prayers. What was disclosed was the value of another human, another individual.

My own approach is more focused on a sexually intimate love that helps to disclose or to awaken and sustain a sense of *our own* value and worth. Love of this sort wakes us up to an appreciation that we too are important and worthy of a special and desirable kind of attention. Even so, I can appreciate the attractiveness of focusing on other kinds of love and the importance of recognizing love's disclosure of the value of others. Humans are, after all, fundamentally egocentric in all sorts of ways: in our reluctance to help those in need, in our complacency and in our unwillingness to leave our comfort zones. Rather than drawing attention to ourselves, it is tempting to hold that the proper direction of attention is always outwards, towards something else, towards whatever is not *us*. Perhaps it is only through such attention that we may hope to rein in our sense of self-importance. It may even seem odd to suggest that we *need* the love of others if we are to fully recognize our own importance.

This is an appealing line of thought, and one that might make any of us uneasy not only about the need to appreciate our own worth but also about the related idea that there is a legitimate kind of self-love. It is also tempting to imagine that the love of self and the love of others must always be mutually incompatible, as if there were a finite quantum of valuing or love to go around, as if any gain to me must be a loss to everyone else. However, there is a distinction that may be drawn here between our default egocentricity and the genuine appreciation of our own worth that results from seeing ourselves in the light of another's love. Default egocentricity is a *preoccupation with* self at the expense of others, but such a preoccupation is entirely consistent with guilt, shame, self-loathing and even masochistic self-hatred. A person might spend a great deal of time thinking about themselves and devote a great deal of attention to themselves without believing they are in any way *worthy* of a better and more desirable form of attention. An appreciation, or just discernment, of our own value in the light of another's love may help us to combat the negative self-images on which a great deal of such egocentricity feeds. Recognizing our own worth in the light of another's love may open us up to the world and to others precisely *because* it relies on the recognition of their authority. It relies on the recognition and acceptance that their judgement counts for something and that we are not the sole arbiters of value. In this respect it helps to situate us within a larger world that is no longer dominated by the self.

Being autonomous and being loved

When I refer to our "being loved" I am using a shorthand for our "actually being loved", or our "previously having been loved" or the belief that either of these is the case. By suggesting that this is, in some sense, necessary for an appropriate appreciation of our own self-worth I am placing myself at odds with a widely held view that is derived from the eighteenth-century German philosopher Immanuel Kant, although at times the reading required to make Kant into a champion of the view in question narrows and distorts his writings to the point where they are barely recognizable. Nonetheless, it does draw on the genuinely Kantian claim that what makes each of us valuable is that we are autonomous rational agents (alternatively, we are "autonomous moral agents"). But it extends this important claim in a problematic way by asserting that *all* we need in order to appreciate our own value is an awareness of this autonomy. Extended in the manner of romantic literature, this view figures in tales where some lone individual holds out against impossible odds, refuses to give in and retains an impregnable sense of their own dignity and worth. Against such a view, we might reflect on all sorts of self-doubts that are intimately associated with the recognition of autonomy. Anxiety, regret and uncertainty seem to go hand in hand with the freedom to make our own choices and with the exercise of our own rational agency. However, love too has problems of the same sort. Its path does not always run smoothly, and this may seem to place autonomy and love on a level footing.

The fundamental problem for an autonomy-based recognition of worth is that, once it is shorn of all heroic trappings, a model of valuing ourselves on this basis fits rather well with some life experiences but poorly with others. It fits well when we are in a position to experience our autonomy as an accomplishment when, for example, we do things for the first time; or when, having escaped from an abusive relationship, we manage to stand on our own two feet; or when, after an illness, we have convalesced and what we then have is autonomy regained and independence accomplished. The sense of having achieved something in these circumstances is both real and familiar.

But an autonomy-focused approach to self-valuing will fit poorly with the experience of someone who has repeatedly failed to find anyone who will love them in the intimate and sexualized way that they want to be loved: someone who has failed to establish even an approximation to an intimate and loving relationship. This, too, is a familiar condition among a section of the very young who are left out of the easy coupling and pairing-off that seems to take place so casually on all sides. The drought may come to an end at some point, but it may go on and on, into their twenties and into their thirties. While I find it appalling to imagine that such failure could go even further, it may be complacent to suppose that things simply *must* improve and that no one will ever be left out. Examples of this sort reinforce the point that a sense of self-worth and egocentricity are very different things. Such circumstances feed egocentricity but undermine and block off a sense of self-worth. Where those in such a predicament have friends but no lovers, the admiration they secure for all manner of accomplishments is liable to be a poor compensation for the seemingly interminable absence of the right kind of love from the right kind of cherished companion.

There are also experiences at the opposite end of a life that fit poorly with the idea that an awareness of autonomy is a sufficient basis for our sense of self-worth. In Iris Murdoch's novel *Bruno's Dream* (1969), there is an illuminating treatment of old age and the combined loss of autonomy and of any sense of being lovable. But it is the latter that is represented as the more dreadful prospect. Murdoch centres her novel on an old man, Bruno, who is confined to his bed, and who has, over the years, become increasingly cut off from others. His sole carer is a son-in-law, the legacy of a marriage to his daughter, but the daughter died long ago. This son-in-law has inherited Bruno just as he has inherited the family printing works, itself an enclosed world with ageing equipment and arcane ways. What exists between these two men is difficult for either to iden-tify as love. Each feels something for the other but if it is a form of love then it is love of a sort that neither can readily acknowledge.

Bruno still retains a good number of his mental faculties. His physical movement is restricted and his deliberative rationality hangs in the balance but he still reasons well enough to torture himself with thoughts about the past, about the son he has alien-ated, the pregnant daughter-in-law that he failed to accept before she suddenly died, and (above all) the wife he betrayed for another woman. Fear of his wife's dreadful reproaches kept Bruno away from her deathbed. Now he is dying and is, for the most part, left alone with his thoughts. Together with a little alcohol in the evening, and a quick glance through his depleted but once impres-sive stamp collection, this is what Bruno's life has become. His greatest torment is not the suffering of a man whose autonomy is all but spent; it is the more dreadful belief that he has become monstrous, an unclean thing, an unlovable being.

In his youth Bruno had the beginnings of a serious and scholarly interest in spiders. In the small room that is the setting for his final days he feels himself to be a withered and tainted creature, all spindly and with an implausibly large head. This is not the normal condition of someone who has outlived others. Bruno has no sense that, had his wife or daughter or daughter-in-law lived, they would now love him. He regards the very thought of their return, and in particular the return of his wife, as one more opportunity for reproach.

In the novel, there is no medical recovery but matters do change and improve. Bruno does not get out of bed and begin to do things for himself but there is a return of love, of a sort, from an unexpected source: from a woman who is brought to the house by his son-in-law. This love is not sexualized and in this and other respects it is similar to the love of Gaita's nun for the patient. But it is, for Bruno, a love that he can recognize and accept with wonder and gratitude. And with it comes the reawakening of his awareness of other possibilities. While sex is no longer an option, *being loved* shows him that he is not physically and morally monstrous: he is not unlovable. With this comes the important half-hope and half-realization that his once-betrayed wife was calling out at the end so that she could forgive him and be with him. At the end he was *wanted*, although he could not see this at the time. Bruno, who has until now been tormented by the past, comes to see it in a new way. This is not redemption but it is consolation, and these two are not the same. It does not undo all the wrongs and untangle the web of his mistakes, but it provides a pathway towards acceptance of fault rather than despair about the self.

One thing the case of Bruno suggests is that we must be ready to acknowledge and to accept the love of others and above all to accept its genuineness, if we ourselves are to be content. While any one of us, as rational agents, may be sceptical about being loved by *this* or *that* person, it is at least tempting to say that a sequential and ongoing scepticism about being loved is unhealthy. Until it is broken or undermined it will impact badly on a life just as it does, for a time, in the case of Bruno. However, it should also be noted that even though love may be more important than autonomy when it comes to the recognition of our own worth, much or all of what has been claimed so far is compatible with the view that humans are of value *because of* our autonomous rational agency, but it also does not rule out other options. At most, it sets up a presumption in favour of the claim that there is more to our value than our rationality. It is, in any case, unlikely that our value could reliably be disclosed to us simply by reflection on our standing as rational agents. It would, after all, be odd for someone who has secured the love of another to shrug their shoulders and say, "I was always aware that I mattered". It would be equally odd for someone who was abandoned by a lover to derive any satisfaction from the reflection "I am still an autonomous rational agent; my value and my awareness of it is utterly undiminished". Love turns out to be too important, too deep and too messy for such utterances to reassure.

Exception-building

While pessimism about the nature of love and a recognition of our need to be loved seem to stand at odds with one another, there is a way in which both can be embraced. It is possible to adopt a qualified or restricted pessimism that is focused on one or more kinds of love while making an exception in the case of love of some other sort. Love is then divided into good and bad, elevated and base, left-handed and right-handed. However, this strategy will only work if the demarcation is secure and the disfavoured love does not return and feed into our understanding of what the favoured love happens to involve.

One way to set up an exception of this sort would be to appeal to the love of friends, for an understanding of which we might turn to Aristotle but probably not to Plato and especially not to Freud. (Plato regards friendship of the best sort as fundamentally erotic; Freud regards it as aim-inhibited sexuality, a covert channelling of our sexual *libido*.) A different option would be to praise parental love, and for this we might look again at Gaita's view of what it is that his nun has mastered as a result of her upbringing. Alternatively, to shed light on the special standing of parental love, we might deliberate about a claim that was once made by Murdoch: that unselfish mothers of large families should be our model of virtue (a model she later abandoned in favour of the love of a childless aunt). But again, for Murdoch, the love in question is best understood as the channelling of our limited erotic resources in a positive, non-egocentric way. The background to this idea of channelling *eros* is that love does not always involve a desire for sexual union but that it may nonetheless be understood as an instance of desire that resembles sexual longing.

Alternatively, to get away from the background influence of both Freudian *libido* and Platonic *eros*, we might look to post-Freudians such as Bowlby, who theorized our evolved need for early recognition and maternal attachment. But if we are ill at ease with a reliance on disputed empirical research, or if we are inclined to reject Bowlby's idea that there is some critical period during which the love of a mother *must* shape our lives if our mental health is later to be sustained, we might then set aside a direct appeal to parental love in favour of what is sometimes called Christian love: a demanding care and readiness to sacrifice self for others, a form of solicitude that is modelled on the love of God or Christ for mankind.

Out of these options I shall focus on the Christian version of exception-building, partly because its appeal to God's love (or to

Christ's love) tends to incorporate some of the more desirable features of the other options: God turns out to be an ideal parent (usually a father) and Christ turns out to be an ideal friend (he'll never let you down). Accordingly, those who are drawn towards the idea that Christian love is our best chance of a love that is free from egocentricity and delusion sometimes excuse a variety of other loves (parental love and the love of friends in particular) while narrowing down the focus of their pessimistic suspicions so that they target only, or primarily, sexualized intimate love for others, a love that does not in any obvious sense exemplify the attitude of God. (God is not a pagan deity with the full range of physical urges.) However, the love of a Christian God, were such a being to exist, would, by definition, escape the familiar charges of egocentricity and delusion more readily than the love of ordinary human parents or the love of ordinary human friends.

As a qualification to what follows, it may also be worth pointing out that the kind of Christian exception-building that I will comment on is not the only way of articulating a Christian account of love, and perhaps it may not be the best way of doing so. There may not even be any best way of articulating a Christian account of love in the light of its canonical texts. What I will attend to is, more simply, what has been maintained, what has been influential and what happens to be relevant to the present discussion. I shall comment on the Christian tradition as a historical phenomenon but I shall not try to track down anything so elusive as the authentic Christian doctrine. If someone should read my comments and remark, "This is not *true* Christianity", I will be happy to reply, "Probably not".

Even so, with or without this qualification, there is an obvious reason why it may seem unhelpful to talk about love of the best sort resembling or being modelled on the love of God. Any such claim may *seem* to require belief in a supernatural agent. However, this is not the case. Talk about a perfect God, or about the perfection of Christ, may be figurative rather than literal. It may involve nothing more objectionable than an appeal to a plausibly inspiring fictional narrative. If we are still uneasy about such talk, we could ultimately translate it into claims of the following sort: we should aspire to love in a way that is modelled on the love that some ideal but fictional observer might have for others. And in this way, no direct appeal to an actual God or to Christ need be made. Tempting though this option is, I shall make no such translation. I shall accept that talk about Christian love captures very well the idea of a special exception to the assumed (broadly delusional) standing of sexualized intimate love and that it does so in a way we can all understand and evaluate on grounds that have nothing to do with God's existence or non-existence. Atheists, agnostics and members of other denominations can all make good sense of the relevant claims without needing to recast them into their own preferred terms. Besides which, appeals to the importance of Christian love are sometimes coupled with a claim about the unique conceptual resources that Christianity alone supplies. While in some respects this is a claim of a sort that any monotheism has to advance in order to set itself apart from other religions, it is not *obviously* a false claim. (It may turn out to be false, but it is not *obviously* so.) It is, at the very least, conceivable that a translation into other terms might risk some unnecessary conceptual loss. To avoid this danger it may be best to work with the familiar vocabulary associated with God, Christianity, God's love, the love of his son, and the relation of both to mankind.

Let us begin a brief exploration of Christian love by considering an instance where it seems to fail. Let us suppose that a young boy does not connect emotionally with the suffering of others as it is depicted on television. He feels disconnected from and indifferent to the plight of a group of children who are shown on-screen, even though they are hungry and clearly in distress. This is not the first time he has been presented with such images. He has seen it all before and has come to the view that the children in question lead a very different kind of life in a distant place. Knowing that he is *supposed* to feel something more and that perhaps others do so, the boy might say to one of his parents, "Why should I care about their feelings? It's all so far away." If the parent in question is a devout Christian, she might reply, "I know it seems remote but we are *all* God's children." In this way, the boy could come to understand that in some respects we are *all* worthy of care and attention and that this is the proper Christian way of looking at matters. With a little thought, the parent's reply might also be taken to imply that everyone is important or that everyone is *equally* important in the way that children are supposed to be equally important to their parents. It could also be taken to imply that God's care for someone gives others a reason to care for them. The parent might reflect on her own words and come to recognize or believe that her response implies some or all of these things, although they may currently be beyond her son's comprehension.

The important claim that "We are all God's children" shows the way in which Christian love may be linked to parental love, as Gaita suggests in his Christian-influenced scenario of the nun who lovingly cares for the patient. It may also be extended into the more problematic claim that our value or worth *comes from* God, that it is one of his many gifts to us or that human life is valuable *only* because we are loved by our creator. The best-known exponent of such a view is the Lutheran theologian Anders Nygren, whose influence stems primarily from the two-volume work *Agape and Eros* (1932–39). Nygren's claim is that Christianity has a unique, or *sui generis*, vocabulary that is embodied in the Bible, more specifically in the New Testament and, somewhat narrowly, in the concept of *agape* (love) that figures repeatedly in the Epistles of St Paul, but which is conspicuously absent elsewhere (the gospels of Matthew, Mark and Luke). This account of *agapaic* Christian love contrasts sharply with any account of love as *eros*, that is, as something that involves or may be understood by analogy with sexual longing. The love in question aspires to caring and to helping but not to sexual coupling. It is probably best known from the following passage in Paul's First Letter to the Corinthians, a passage that falls immediately after the claim that without love our lives will be hollow:

> Love is patient, love is kind *and* is not jealous; love does not brag *and* is not arrogant, does not act unbecomingly; it does not seek its own, is not provoked, does not take into account a wrong *suffered*, does not rejoice in unrighteousness, but rejoices with the truth; bears all things, believes all things, hopes all things, endures all things.
>
> (New Standard American Bible: 1 Corinthians 13.4–7)

Nygren is not blind to the fact that *agape* happens to be used in a variety of senses by Paul, sometimes in ways that makes it interchangeable with *philia*, an older Greek term for a variety of loves including the love that is involved in friendship. But he identifies what he believes to be a dominant sense that separates it out both as imitative of God's love for man and as a love that is radically desexualized. Beyond this love, nothing is allowed to be genuinely Christian, "God's Agape is the criterion of Christian love. Nothing but that which bears the impress of Agape has a right to be called Christian love" (Nygren 1969: 92). This may allow for the possibility that a relationship with an *erotic* dimension could still involve Christian love. Nygren is not suggesting that marriage, which after all is bound up with sex, is unchristian. But any relationship that includes such an *erotic* component could only involve Christian love for the quite different reason that it also has some other, and quite different, *agapaic* component. However, at times it is difficult to see how the two could coexist given that they belong to what Nygren calls "two entirely separate spiritual worlds, between which no direct communication is possible" (*ibid.*: 31–2).

As a further clarification, what may make sense here is *not* the suggestion that anyone could actually love in a way that is directly imitative of the love of God (who knows everyone intimately and hence cannot encounter strangers) but rather the claim that we should all try to love as he would do if he were an embodied being like us. That is to say, we should love in the unconditional and desexualized or non-erotic manner of Christ. Minimally, such a view requires that all humans are suitable recipients of this special kind of love and that if we cannot actually love everyone we should at least strive to love those we know. In more familiar terms, we should love our neighbour. This position is not difficult to understand but it *is* fairly demanding

Nygren's explanation of why *everyone* is equally suitable as a recipient of such love is that it is not a response to any independently conceived human merit or worth. God's love is not constrained by any prior facts about human importance:

> God does not love that which is already in itself worthy of love, but on the contrary, that which in itself has no worth acquires worth just by becoming the object of God's love. Agape has nothing to do with the kind of love that depends on the recognition of a valuable quality in its object; Agape does not recognize value but creates it.   (*Ibid.*: 78)

This is stronger than a suggestion of divine indifference to independent human value that might be rooted in our rationality or elsewhere, in our standing as feeling and suffering mortal beings. If taken literally, it states that humans *become* valuable only and precisely because God loves us and we remain valuable only because of this love. For those who are not committed Christians, and even for many Christians, this can be a deeply unattractive view.

For others, and in particular those Christians who wish to understand as much as possible in a God-centred way, it can be a welcome message that plays on a recurring theme. It is a theme that we may associate on the one hand with monastic figures such as Saint Benedict and Bernard of Clairvaux and, on the other, with at least some instances of Christian fundamentalism. The former articulate Christianity in a way that emphasizes humility as an important virtue (which it is), but they also regard it as a virtue of self-abnegation, an acceptance by mortal beings that we are mere *dust* or *nothing* in comparison to God. The kind of self-abnegation in question is quite different from spiritual exercises that happen to involve the cautious use of an imagery of personal unimportance, and different also from what is sometimes called "unselfing", in the sense of a practice that involves abandoning egocentric illusions about ourselves (Milligan 2007). It is also a form of abnegation that is rejected by prominent Christian figures such as Thomas Aquinas. However, it makes our value dependent on God in a way that is looked on favourably by fundamentalists. And while their tone and intolerance may be utterly unlike Nygren's gentle and scholarly Christianity, the all-encompassing importance that both ascribe to God threatens to silence any claims about humans being important *because we are humans*.

An example may illustrate the point. In 1983 a group of fundamentalist Christian parents in Hawkins County, Tennessee attempted to have their children made exempt from the use of schoolbooks containing exercises that they deemed unacceptable. In one reading exercise a boy cooks while a girl reads to him (a disregard for what the parents saw as the natural, God-given difference between the sexes). In another, there is brief reportage of a central idea of the Renaissance, "a belief in the dignity and worth of all human beings". The parents regarded this as incompatible with mankind's utter dependence on God (Gutmann & Thompson 1996: 63–4). In a test case that sometimes figures in philosophical treatments of the importance of deliberation as a part of democracy, the parents' request was turned down. Nonetheless, their stand on the question of human worth exemplifies a persistent tendency on the part of those who wish to situate God at the heart of all things. In a sense, the parents were quite right. Their values were being challenged in the classroom.

Even so, the idea of Christian love may be disentangled from any such fundamentalism and from a territorially aggressive conception of God's importance. Nygren's account may also be varied so that an initial value-bestowing act by God is seen as a historical myth: a fictional endorsement of our *de facto* possession of worth that does *not* result from any arbitrary human choice and cannot therefore be eliminated by shifting moods, changing times or the unpopularity of a minority population whose value has been placed in question. On a charitable appraisal, we may suspect that this was always Nygren's intention.

Problems with a rigid *agape/eros* distinction

But even when Nygren's version of Christian love is understood or reworked in a generous and qualified manner, we may feel uneasy both about the account itself and about what motivates it. That is to say, *I* feel uneasy about it and I do so, in part, because his distinction involves an attitude that was plausibly criticized by Freud. While I do not buy into the entirety of Freud's explanatory machinery (which, after all, does involve a different kind of pessimism about the nature of love), I cannot help reflecting on the plausibility of his critique of the distinction between love that is elevated and love that is debased or, in other terms, love that is sacred and love that is profane. A stable feature of Freud's otherwise shifting account of human development is that there is a time in our growth as individuals during which sexual desire is latent and affection manifest (affection for parents, siblings and friends). On the Freudian account, the re-emergence of overt sexuality during puberty then poses a dilemma. We can integrate it with feelings of affection that we direct towards new "love objects" and what then results is the familiar, slightly delusional, but comparatively unproblematic, love of a partner. Or we can fail to integrate sexual desire and affection, in which case the sexual desire does not go away but remains in isolation. We then have to live a divided life with an unbridgeable gulf between our denigrated sexuality and our deceptively pure loving affection. In its more extreme forms, particularly in the case of men, the result is that our sexual *libido* is not only channelled in two different ways but is also directed towards what we (quite mistakenly) believe to be two different kinds of object. The result (again in the case of men) is that we separate out women into Madonnas, who are to be worshipped but not touched, and whores, who are suitable objects for our debased and debasing sexual longings (Freud 1984: 231–42).

In its broadest features, this looks like a suspiciously realistic description of a familiar and all too real attitude that is closely allied to those versions of Christianity that are uncomfortable about sex. It also looks like a suspiciously realistic description of what may result whenever spiritual practices *of whatever sort* (Christian or otherwise) are taken to require voluntary celibacy during the time when affection and overt sexual longing usually start to merge. But those who are uneasy about this appeal to Freud, given that he did not always have a good feel for spiritual life, may prefer to think of the same problem in a different way. From time to time I have suggested to students that they might approach Nygren's rigid division between *agape* and *eros* by thinking about Titian's painting *Sacred and Profane Love* (*circa* 1514), on the understanding that Titian is someone who did have a deep and substantial grasp of human spirituality, albeit one that was not unambiguously Christian.

The title of the painting is a convenient addition dating from around a century later, but it is easy to see why the association with the distinction between the sacred and the profane was quickly made and has stuck. To one side of the canvas sits an opulently dressed woman (not always a sign of respectability in early-modern Venice). Her hands are gloved, placing her beyond a capacity for touch. Her contact with the viewer, and more specifically with a presupposed male viewer, is strictly visual. She sees and is seen. Towards the other side of the canvas sits a woman who is naked apart from a flowing crimson robe and a simple covering that is draped over her genitalia and upper thighs. While the clothed woman looks out at the viewer, the naked woman sits slightly higher and looks instead at a cherub-like Eros who plays between them. It is tempting to say that the purer and more innocent vision of beauty is the naked woman rather than the clothed one. She is more elevated and more disconnected from us. But look again and you will see that both appear to be suspiciously like a single woman who is represented in different ways. At the very least, each could take the place of the other without in any way unsettling the composition of the painting. It is the viewer who may be deluded into regarding each as a woman who must determinately be one thing or the other, as if a woman could not be many things together in one life or could not be a spiritual being *through* her eroticism, through her loving and Eros-directed gaze.

What makes Nygren suspicious about this kind of attempt to link eroticism and spirituality is that it owes something to classical pagan ideas about spiritual life, about our standing as sexual beings and about the inseparability of both. However, for many Christians, this is a bad place to draw a clear dividing line between the Christian tradition and classical paganism. Nygren's critics have also been quick to point out that, in the past, the Christian tradition has been only too willing to deploy sexual imagery and to appeal to longing and desire, not as an *aside* to what spiritual life involves, but rather as a central aspect of Christian love. This is particularly obvious in the case of the love that humans are supposed to have for God, a love that is always taken to involve a need or longing and so is, in this and perhaps other respects, *erotic*. Nygren accepts this as a difficult-to-ignore feature of the Christian tradition but regards it as a confusion introduced from the outside, a confusion that obscures the central motif of true Christian doctrine as it is embodied in the relevant primary texts.

But here we may wonder whether there is any confusion at all. In what is perhaps the most widely read twentieth-century work on the different components of Christian love, C. S. Lewis makes the remark: "Every Christian would agree that a man's spiritual health is exactly proportional to his love for God. But man's love for God, from the very nature of the case, must always be very largely, and must often be entirely, a Need-love" (1964: 8). This comment is not an attempt by Lewis to dispute the importance of love that is a Christ-like gift; rather, it is part of his determination to dispute the radical separability of what he calls "Need-love" and the "Gift-love" that is exemplified in the life and teachings of Christ.

As a way around the problem it may be tempting to distinguish between a Christ-like *agapaic* love for our fellow humans and a human love of God, which admittedly is best understood by appeal to erotic imagery. This would keep *agape* clear of any direct association with sexuality and the erotic. We would then simply love humans in one way and love God in another. But there is a problem here, a problem identified in Pope Benedict's first encyclical *Deus Caritas Est* (1996), with its insistence that a rigid *agape/eros* dichotomy threatens any understanding of spiritual life as a continuous, moment-to-moment lived experience:

Were this antithesis to be taken to extremes, the essence of Christianity would be detached from the vital relations fundamental to human existence, and would become a world apart, admirable perhaps, but decisively cut off from the complex fabric of human life. (2006: 24)

As a clarifying question it is worth asking, how can a Christian love God *except* by loving others? Perhaps we might imagine that the love of God could involve such things as private acts of prayer, longing and contemplation. but this is Christianity of a rarefied sort. It is not Christianity that embeds the love of God in an everyday care for others. In this respect, it is also difficult to regard it as a plausible imitation of Christ.

An alternative to Nygren's approach has been at work within Christianity for a very long time. It is an option that is made explicit by Kierkegaard and by the influential French philosophical mystic Simone Weil. It involves a claim that the love of neighbours, of nature and of others is *indirectly* a form of love for God. As remarked in the previous chapter, for Kierkegaard it is precisely *this* ongoing everyday relation to the divine that makes love "deep". Weil focuses on neighbour-love and nature-love, but Kierkegaard suggests that the same point extends to any kind of love, including the sexualized intimate love that exists between couples. When I first encountered this claim about an indirect love some years ago, in the small collection of extracts from Weil's notebooks known as *Waiting for God* (1951), I was uneasy about it. Weil seemed to be suggesting that love is never really *about* the other human (although it *can*, egocentrically or narcissistically, be about ourselves). In retrospect, I misunderstood a great many things that Weil was saying, partly because she says so many things and some of them jar with one another. But I do not think that my reservation was entirely based on a misunderstanding. Weil's position has its roots in her reading of Plato and in particular it is rooted in his idea that love for one thing *must* displace love for something else (Weil 1952: 280; Plato, *Republic* 485d–e). It is this view that ultimately leads Plato to suspect that, in spite of its wonders, human love may be second-rate in comparison with love of something other and higher, a love that exceeds our understanding.

The same problematic either/or attitude that allows us to love one thing only at the expense of another is also present in Kierkegaard:

> As soon as a love-relationship does not lead me to God, and as soon as I in a love-relationship do not lead another person to God, this love, even if it were the most blissful and joyous attachment, even if it were the highest good in the lover's earthly life, nevertheless is not true love. The world can never get through its head that God in this way not only becomes the third party in every relationship of love but essentially becomes the only loved object, so that it is not the husband who is the wife's beloved, but it is God. (2009: 125)

Understood in the terms that Kierkegaard favours, Christian love both is territorially ambitious (whenever atheists love they must love God without being aware of doing so) *and* dovetails problematically with attempts to set up a pessimism about the nature of love by claiming that our love is not about those we believe it to be about and that their love is not ultimately about us. If reformulation is allowed, these problems need not be intractable. I have already committed to the view that emotions such as love have mixed intentionality. Characteristically, they are about more than one thing, even when there is a clear sense in which they are focused on an immediately present individual. Given this, there seems little reason to object to the idea of an indirect love of God, just so long as the account of such love is reformulated to allow that it is genuinely about its indirect object and still about its direct object, which will often be some other human. In this way, a story can be told that allows Christian love to have inseparable *agapaic* and *erotic* dimensions. But the resulting conception of Christian love no longer counts as an attempt to combine a qualified pessimism about the nature of love with an exercise in exception-building.

In line with this approach, we may read Gaita's example of the nun who cares lovingly for the patient in the following way: it is *both* an instance of loving another human (without desiring them sexually) *and* an instance of Christian religious devotion to God (a love that is best understood in erotic terms). This might even make sense of the nun's way of seeing matters. But, as Kierkegaard notes, the idea that the love of others is an indirect way of relating to God works equally well with the parent's love of their child, the love of friends for each other, and with the love between husband and wife (to which list we may add the love between intimate sexual partners). Perhaps it is because I am not a Christian that I find this account of Christian love more attractive than Nygren's equation of the latter with a comprehensively desexualized love. Perhaps I find it more appealing because I do not understand well enough what it is like to *be* a Christian. But others who regard themselves as Christians have also found this an attractive option. Consider the following way of making the same point. A mother with a number of young children to look after finds that there are not enough hours in the day to allow her to go regularly to church. One minister pops around and suggests that she should get up an hour earlier in order to attend mass. Another pops around and tries to get her to recognize that her loving care for the children can itself be a form of religious devotion, a way of loving God, and one that is all the more significant because it involves caring about what he cares about. This is a love that is not cut off from the rest of her daily life. It does not put spirituality in a corner (Soskice 1992).

An approach of this sort fuses various kinds of love, including love that is directly sexual and love that is in some other sense erotic, as well as the benevolent love of neighbours, into a complex conception of what it takes to love in a Christian manner. But care may still need to be taken to formulate this account of Christian love in a modest way that is not territorially ambitious and does not stamp itself down as a requirement on all true love. To say "Love *can* reach out in a way that involves an implicit or indirect love of God" is very different from asserting "Love, even by non-Christians, *must* or *ought to* reach out in a way that involves an implicit or indirect love of God". Perhaps it is still true that the love of two people for each other *always* reaches out and is never strictly a two-sided relation. But even if this is the case it is not obvious that such love must always reach out in the same way to a further, single and unitary something else (God, the transcendent, a unitary Good, and so on). It may instead spill over in all sorts of directions that depend on the personal and shared histories of the two lovers in question.

There may also be a concern about the appropriateness of a Christian love for our neighbours if such a love is understood to be unconditional or, less attractively, indiscriminate. Some neighbours may have committed dreadful acts that fill us with a sense of moral horror. Perhaps the Christian God could still love them; I do not find it odd to say that he could still love Hitler and Jack the Ripper given that God would not be their neighbour but would always be *in loco parentis* and that parents often cannot help loving their children. However, it seems like *hubris*, like an overreaching of what is appropriate to humans, to imitate love of this sort and, in doing so, to love, and hence desire the well-being of, those who have committed such deeds. Such a love could not plausibly be a moral requirement. It is also difficult to see why it would be a good thing.

On a more positive note, there need be no concern that a neighbourly Christian love by those who have no desire for sex with us must always fail to awaken us to a sense of our own value. There are many among us, forgotten and neglected individuals who in some respects resemble Murdoch's Bruno, who may find that being loved in such a way can help to reignite a sense of self-worth. But for the rest of us, even if we remain open to the possibility of such neighbourly love, it is often not the kind of love that we most want. And when we are fortunate enough to share an intimate sexualized love with another, it may not seem to be a love that we need.

5. Togetherness and loss

I have tried to make sense of the idea that love is a deep part of human life. In doing so I have advanced a number of discrete but interrelated claims, such as: the claim that sexualized intimate love is a good exemplar of love in general; that love involves seeing others as unique but doing so in the light of our own history; and that, for our own well-being, we need at some time in our lives to be loved because nothing else discloses our value and worth in quite the same way. The guiding, but so far unstated, assumption behind this rather piecemeal approach is that nothing works as a complete theory of everything that we are inclined to call "love". Another way to make the same point would be to say that love is, in some respects, mysterious. The elusiveness of a complete theory may have something to do with the absence of any plausible and complete account of the emotions in general, or with the fact that, if we think of love as an emotion, it will turn out to be an emotion that is somewhat anomalous. The elusiveness of a complete theory of love may also be related to love's depth. There are deep aspects of ourselves that humans have always found uncanny or slightly beyond our comprehension.

As well as holding back from a complete theory of love, I have also tried to avoid presenting a complete theory of what love's depth involves. Instead, I have explored only some of the more obvious ways in which it *is* deep. Others, who do not share my philosophical temperament, will no doubt find this approach unsatisfactory and perhaps even frustrating. They may yearn for a more comprehensive account that says "Love is x" or "Love is x plus y plus z". And perhaps someone may eventually come along and provide a theory of love that is set out in just this manner and it will be in every way satisfactory. My assumption about love's mysteriousness will then look rather naive or unduly influenced by a mistaken conception of human life. I take this to be a minor risk, and unimportant in the larger scale of things. It is the price that must be paid for saying what I want to say. And part of what I want to say is that having a number of important insights about love is not at all the same thing as having a complete and final theory, even if we choose to regard such insights as a step towards such a theory (which I do not).

To regard love as in *some* respects mysterious is not the same as claiming that it cannot be analysed in *any* respect or that we cannot identify important features that are always present in love irrespective of the kind of love that is in question. Those who have a fondness, or a weakness, for formalizing matters in a rigorous manner (as I do, on occasion) can still explore significant claims. They (we) can still comment on the truth of the following: "If X loves Y then it is the case that X is vulnerable to Y-related harm"; or "If X loves Y then it is the case that X desires that Y should escape extreme suffering"; or "If X loves Y then X desires to be with Y". Long afternoons can be devoted to building up a list of such claims. Time spent in the exercise might lead to a pared-back version of the ideas that I explore below, but again they should not be mistaken for an account of everything we could ever want to know about love.

Accepting the mysteriousness of love also need not remove our enquiry too far from an everyday appreciation of what love involves. The problem of setting aside our experience, and becoming, instead, rather vague about love through imprecise forms of praise, is a persistent danger in certain kinds of discourse, particularly those that are open to the idea that *in some sense* love has a spiritual dimension (an assumption that need not require any supernatural apparatus to support it). The danger of drifting away from our familiarity with love in everyday contexts is present when it is suggested that love of the best sort or *the only true or pure love,* is an imitation of God's love or of Christ's love for mankind. The same danger is present in Plato's very unchristian account of love as the offspring of guile and need, a trickster who lures us unwittingly into knowledge. Plato suggests that desire (*eros*) leads the truest and most persistent lover onwards and upwards, from an initial longing to be in the presence of their beloved towards a longing for pure beauty and (we may surmise) a longing for the pure goodness that is closely allied to beauty. This is all very nice, but there is a danger that the tangible and the familiar may be lost. More particularly, there is a danger that a robustly sexualized form of caring for another may be displaced by a supposedly higher and more spiritually elevated conception of love that is only a bloodless imitation of the real thing.

Plato has his own way of warning the reader about this danger in the *Symposium.* The guests at his dinner party are represented setting out a succession of accounts of love, each more uplifting than the last. Love is described as more than bodily attraction: it is the recognition of one soul for another; a recognition of the beauty that all souls possess; a longing for the same beauty that can be found in intellectual endeavours. Ultimately, this strange and thrilling *eros* draws or lures us towards a desire for beauty in its own right, quite apart from any particular beautiful things or individual beautiful people. But, as the guests are contemplating these noble images, there is a rude knocking at the door. In pours Alcibiades, beautiful, bold and drunk. He tells the tale of his failed attempt to seduce Socrates. The episode has been understood in many ways, but I am firmly on the side of those who read it as Plato's way of bringing us back down to earth: a way of reminding us that he too is a dealer in shadows and images, a constructor of artful representations of the real rather than a purveyor of the real itself or, even better, what he elsewhere calls the "really real". This is a timely reminder to keep the recognition of love's mysteriousness within touching distance of our familiar and accessible experience of what love is like: to keep it in touch with love's known desires and with the experienced physicality of the erotic. And here I continue to use "erotic" as a broad label for anything sexual or anything that may be understood by analogy with sexual desire.

At least part of the time, in a long relationship, love may be something that works away in the background, unobtrusive and unnoticed, like a silent part of our being. But there are times, when we fall in love, when we begin to fall out of love or when we *lose* those we love, when its presence is clear, obvious and even visceral. On these occasions life can have an intensity that we cannot cope with for any prolonged period of time. But, to a greater or lesser extent, love of any sort, and at any time, can have a solidly *affective* dimension. That is to say, it can have an impact on us in a sheer and bodily manner. Here I do not simply mean that it can cause a swelling of the genitals, although I *do* mean that too. It is part of Plato's genius that he manages to direct our *attention* to this experienced physicality of love even in the midst of a text that conveys a strong overall sense of love's mystery and a sense that love points beyond the partnership of humans. He does something similar in the *Phaedrus*, a later dialogue on a similar theme. The reader is told that the written word is unreliable and that the lover of beauty is someone who begins to feels their wings unfurl. But just when we expect a flight into the intangible, Plato inserts a series of the most blatantly sexual images. The opening of our wings involves "shuddering", "high-fever", "melting", "throbbing", "palpitating", "aching" and "growing" as the wings come to life (*Phaedrus* 251a). Of course, Plato was a genius and the rest of us have to make do with a less dramatic mode of presentation, but even an enquiry that lacks his artistry may find ways to strike a balance between doing justice to love's mystery and doing justice to what we all know and are familiar with.

Love's desires

In calling on Platonic imagery to make sense of the experience of love, my concern is not simply to draw attention to sexual desire. My concern is with love's *erotic* dimension more generally, that is, with the kind of desire that may under some circumstances involve us in sheer physical longing. Sexual desire happens to be a particularly good example of this, but there are other kinds of longing that are not, in an everyday sense, sexual. There is the longing of a parent for their child when the child is known to be in great danger and the longing that we all experience when we are grief-stricken and struggling to accept that the person we love is lost to us forever.

Longing of this sort is an occasional condition but it results from desires that are an ongoing feature of love and not merely their familiar accompaniment. The desires in question are partly *constitutive* of what love is, irrespective of the kind of love in question. To talk in this way about love as partly a matter of *desiring* (as well as *seeing* and *needing*) has often been a source of unease. If the desires in question concern ourselves then they may readily be dismissed as egocentric. Freud and Proust both believed something along these lines: that love is part of a private drama conducted within the self. But if instead the desires concern the well-being of the other person, the person we love, then they may involve all sorts of dispositions to do things on their behalf and generally to get in the way of their autonomy and independence. Like the attitude of a devoted but fussy parent, or of a son or daughter who cares for an ageing relative, a benevolent attitude may be intrusive. Whether welcome or unwelcome, such love is problematic. It can also be a way of acting out our own fears and anxieties rather than a way of addressing the needs of the other person. And this, to some extent, returns us to the idea that egocentricity may be at work.

But even if love's desires are truly about the other person, there is a further concern that these desires may conflict with our duties to society at large. Consider again the case of what it is to love an ageing relative, but this time factor in the importance of the relative's ability to get out. Let us suppose that they habitually drive everywhere, associate their compromised independence with doing so, and that they would be uncomfortable and ill at ease if required to travel in any other way. Faced with the prospect of losing their car they would probably stay indoors. Now let us assume that they are liable to be a menace on the roads or, more ambiguously, that they have had a series of small accidents for which they find it difficult to accept any responsibility. Perhaps they say, "The roads are full of terrible drivers", but the drivers in question are always taken to be other people. Nobody has been hurt so far, but partly this is a matter of luck. At some time the prospect of such a relative driving will be intolerable. Do you try to convince them to give up their car *now*, knowing that if they do so it will in all likelihood accelerate their decline? Do you ignore the queries about health, dizziness and memory problems when you help them to fill in the driving licence renewal form? These are real and lived dilemmas. The temptation to consider their interests at the expense of others may be powerful.

Similar considerations apply in the case of sexualized intimate love. Perhaps my life would be simpler if I could drive. This may be known to my wife or at least she might believe it to be the case. But my attempts to drive have convinced both myself and Suzanne that the world will be a safer place if I continue to use public transport. She does not encourage me to make my life simpler and easier at the expense of the rest of the world, or at the expense of those portions of the world that might otherwise be at risk.

Less dramatically, intimately involved couples tend to support each other even when they are in the wrong. The fact that someone is loved, and that we desire their well-being, does not mean they cannot harm or be unfair to others. Here I am tempted to say that there can be more than one kind of reason for acting and that the reasons for acting out of love may sometimes be just as legitimate as those we associate with a more impersonal sense of duty, even when the two kinds of reasons happen to conflict. Sometimes duty trumps love and sometimes love trumps duty. We all know this even if, on particular occasions, we find it hard to accept.

If we are concerned about the idea that love and duty can pull us in different directions, or about the danger of egocentric desires, or if we simply value autonomy over all else, we may then be tempted to downplay the role of desire in love or even to deny that it is a built-in feature of love at all. This will make love look like a pleasantly impersonal and altruistic attitude rather than something that may be understood by analogy with sex or with sexual longing. One way of making this move is to suggest that desire is merely a camp follower rather than a part of love's regular forces. On such an account, when we love we may often *happen* to desire or, when we love, we desire as a result of the love, but the desire itself is not the stuff the love is made of. Love may then be something pure and recognitional, the discernment of the other person's dignity or selfhood, or something else of this sort. In recent years, this view has been associated with the American philosopher David Velleman.

This is not a view with which I have any great sympathy. I accept the familiar claim that when we love someone, in whatever way, we *want* them to flourish or at least we *desire* that things go reasonably well for them and that they come to no great harm. We may, from time to time, desire that something bad, unfortunate or at least inconvenient happens to friends, relatives and partners, or we may want them to learn some lesson the hard way, but this is consistent with desiring that, overall, things go well and that those we love may escape from life's more damaging episodes. From time to time I want Suzanne to mess something up. When I am perched precariously at the top of a ladder and demonstrating that I know less about painting than I know about the composition of the sun, I may want Suzanne to discover that her advice is no good or that it comes a bit late in the day. From time to time she probably wishes me to see how foolish I have been and there are occasions on which she is probably wise to do so. I have no desire to live with someone who lacks edge or insight into my faults. A rather clever, flesh and blood woman will do me just fine. But our attitudes change as soon as matters get serious. We are on each other's side.

There is, however, something more and deeper than partisanship, sympathy or altruism at work in a love of this sort. A well-wisher to whom neither of us has any personal relation might call down joy upon our house but our connection to such a person would be, in some respects, tenuous. We could not, without further and closer acquaintance, feel for them in the same way that we feel for each other. Our love, like that of any intimate lovers, emerges out of a shared past. Although any of us may feel love's first stirrings at an early stage in a relationship, intimate love that is genuine and reciprocated is a response to a shared history. As a result of such a history, our own desires and the desires of the person that we love become entangled. My desires for Suzanne's well-being have become entangled with my desires for my own well-being. But this does not make them covertly suspect. It would be wrong to suggest that what is involved here is an egocentric conception of intimacy. I do not desire good things for Suzanne simply as a means to fulfil my own plans and to make myself happy. What I desire is my happiness, her happiness and our happiness. All three are related.

Those who love one another in a sexualized manner delight in each other's company (some or most of the time) and in the experience of various sorts of physical intimacy. In the context of such a relationship, physical togetherness and sex may be recognized as things that join and bind. Sex in particular can build trust through the acceptance of vulnerability, through a sharing of experience and through a mixing of desires for our own pleasure with desires for the pleasure of the other person. Here, although the direct example I have in mind is my life with Suzanne, I allude also to a Platonic image mentioned earlier: the image of the severed halves of some greater being who find one another after many years and rush to fuse and join. They seek to heal an ancient wound by returning to a lost unity of being. It is an image that Plato finds arresting but at the same time problematic.

Whatever its faults, it has considerable resonance and particularly so in my own case. When I was married to Suzanne we faced each other and made our vows about what we would try to do and about the ways in which we expected to fall short. We were handfasted, tied with cords, forearm to forearm, with bindings chosen to symbolize passion, good intent and the fact that we were part of a larger natural world. Out of respect for ourselves and for each other we made no claims of an impossible sort or promises that could not be kept. In a sense, although our vows were not chosen with Plato in mind, we addressed his concern that love should not be made to bear any impossible burdens, should not be allowed to appear capable of healing all wounds and overcoming all human limitations and weakness.

But a ceremony such as a handfasting, a symbolic joining together of lovers, might readily be regarded as all show and performance. It would be an *agelast*, an enemy of human laughter and warmth, who refused to allow couples to indulge in some light fantasy on such an occasion. Other people prefer to dress as characters from *Star Trek* or turn up in fairytale dresses and pumpkin-shaped carriages. On a wedding day such things are allowed. A little more generously, a ceremony of joining might be understood *only* as a celebration of the limited joining together of sexual union, which in part it is, rather than the outward and visible symbol of a shared identity or, more simply, the sharing of a life. A ceremony of joining might be challenged by those who have no poetry in their souls as the perpetration of an illusion upon the gullible. There can, after all, be no real and ultimate joining of persons, not even by surgical means. The determined *agelast* and the image-smashing puritan might also object to any symbol of joining together as an affront to human dignity and autonomy. They may point out that no one should imagine that they can or ought to give up their separateness and that no one ought to compromise the autonomy and separateness of others. Even seeking to do so may seem to involve a fault.

I accept that it is difficult to understand the sense in which separate humans can be joined together, the sense in which a couple can share a life rather than simply *being* in many of the same places at the same time. But I do not suggest that *this* aspect of love is altogether mysterious. Nor is it uncontroversial. Irving Singer, who knows more about theories of love than perhaps anyone else alive, regards the imagery and the idea of joining or merging as both deep and suspect. In a passage that is vaguely reminiscent of Stendhal's acceptance that love involves a necessary illusion, he remarks:

> I am not suggesting that one shouldn't even think about merging. The *thought* of it is an integral feature of our mentality as creative beings, inasmuch as it issues from speculation that makes us inventive and imaginative. But the concept itself is not true to our reality, what we are as human beings. The nature of love must therefore be elucidated in other, less fanciful ways. (2009: 27)

Togetherness

I want to suggest that the image of joining or of merging is truer to our reality than Singer's comment allows. And what I have to say may be slightly offensive to those who prize autonomy above all things. For what it is worth, I tend to think of autonomy as important *to some extent* and *up to a point*, but love is at least as important. I am tempted to say that in a good life, a balance must be maintained between the two, but perhaps this too would be misleading. There may be a case for saying that love and togetherness shape autonomy rather than weighing against it. And even an acceptance that the imagery of striking a balance may be appropriate is not the same as the belief that such a balance is easy to achieve. There are occasions on which a concern for love and a concern for autonomy may lead us to see matters in competing ways. It seems difficult to deny that on some occasions love can conflict with autonomy just as it can conflict with a sense of duty. A concern for love may lead us to favour one course of action while a concern for our independence may lead us to act in a quite different way. Having to sacrifice one or the other is a dilemma of a sort that is so familiar that it could hardly be called tragic. In the present context, a concern for autonomy may support Singer's suspicion about the imagery of joining together, but a concern for love may lead us to view the imagery with more sympathy.

Genuine and reciprocated love involves sharing, but not in the way that business partners share their premises. Something more intimate and personal goes on, something more akin to the sharing of a life. And this is precisely what the imagery of joining together suggests even if imaginative representations of joining may sometimes overstate matters. Those who love each other in an intimate way come to share not only time, location and activities, but also *desires*. And here I am suggesting *more* than the often-mistaken idea that lovers come to be fond of the same things. If Suzanne and I happened to share the same taste in music, clothes, chocolate or coffee (which we don't) this would hardly amount to an intimate bond that was worthy of note. As things stand, our taste in such matters overlaps and diverges but this gives neither of us a good reason to question the genuineness or depth of our own love or to lapse into some form of scepticism about being loved.

A slightly more interesting suggestion is that people who love one another are of a single mind on various issues *because* they trust each other's judgement. And it is the "because" here that is the issue and the sticking point. Again, in some cases this is true, but in others the claim breaks down. For example, Suzanne has a fondness for crisps, rockumentaries and soap operas that are set in hospitals. I want her to enjoy these things but I do not share her judgement about their merits. I do not automatically trust that her desires about trivial matters are well directed or that I would be in any way happier if I began to desire these same things. And this is *not* because I regard desires about trivial matters as non-rational or arbitrary or subjective in the sense of only ever being a matter of individual taste. And, oddly enough, there may be a sense in which the having of desires about trivial matters may be important. (It involves a particular kind of engagement with the things that surround us.) But I don't see the need to trust Suzanne's judgement about trivial matters or for her to trust mine.

There is a better and more straightforward way of cashing out the idea that intimate love leads to shared desires. The fact that Suzanne desires something gives me a good reason to desire it even though it may be a defeasible reason: a reason that may be over-ridden by other considerations such as the recognition that *she doesn't consider it all that important*. But even in cases where her desire is stronger, she might still desire something that would harm her. I might be aware of this danger and she might not. As a result we would not end up desiring the same thing. Alternatively, some desire that I have may be so outlandish that Suzanne may simply find it difficult to share, or she may happen to desire something that requires knowledge and interest in a subject that I know nothing about. In all sorts of ways the sharing of desires, and particularly the sharing of our unimportant desires that we do not identify with *who we are*, can be blocked.

Nonetheless, the fact that Suzanne desires something still gives me at least one defeasible *reason* to desire it, and particularly so when the desire in question does happen to be connected to her sense of identity. And this reason is *my desire that she be happy*. I want a great many of the same things that she wants precisely because I want her life to go well and, whatever else this involves, a good number of her desires, and particularly her core or identity and value-expressing desires, must be satisfied if this is to happen. Desire fulfilment in these cases may not be *all* that is required for someone's life to go well, but it is still an important part of the story. It would, after all, be hard to make sense of a life of persistent desire-frustration as anything other than unpleasant.

While a benevolent stranger who wishes joy on our house might also desire that Suzanne's life goes well, they will have no particular reason to share her desires as opposed to sharing the (perhaps incompatible) desires of the other people towards whom they also happen to have a benevolent attitude. In any case, they will lack a detailed awareness of what her well-being would involve. At best they may fill in the blanks by hoping that she gets *some of the things she wants* or *what humans want* or *what women in general want*. Such a well-wisher would be poorly placed to share her desires in the intimately informed way that I can share them. It is not simply that the well-wisher would know nothing about the crisps, the soap operas and all the rest. They would also have no particular insight into the desires that Suzanne regards as part of the complex fibre of her being or the way in which her everyday practices, even practices as seemingly simple as eating, express these desires and also express her sense of what is important.

When I first began to eat with Suzanne a potential barrier quickly emerged. She was already a vegetarian and although I admired vegetarianism and held the view that one day, in a better and future world, humans would probably be vegetarians, I did very little about it. I did not regard diet as a priority. Then one day as we sat in the downstairs section of the Barnton Bar and Bistro in Stirling, two meals duly arrived: something veggie for Suzanne and a smallish hunk of meat for me. The meat was covered in a blackcurrant sauce that looked a little too much like blood. At this point it was obvious that something would have to give. If my memory serves me well, I decided there and then, or at least shortly after the meal, that it was time to give vegetarianism a go.

In retrospect, perhaps I wanted to ingratiate myself. But this may not be the whole story. I genuinely didn't want to eat the meat in front of her and I certainly didn't want to start covert and secretive meat-eating. And I already held clear but poorly supported views about vegetarianism being a good practice. Suzanne made no request that I change my diet. She seemed prepared to put up with my being a carnivore. But *putting up with* is hardly the best option. On this matter, concerning a value-expressing practice, it struck me as important that we should not be at odds, particularly when she was probably right, and not because she tended to be right or trustworthy about absolutely everything but because of the issue in question. In retrospect, what mattered was not the sheer activity of meat-eating but rather the values and desires that our respective diets expressed. It would, for example, have been no good for me to stop eating meat (even in solitary moments) while secretly longing for it. What needed to go was not only the behaviour involved in meat-eating but also the desire to eat meat. First I abandoned the practice and then, a surprisingly short time afterwards, the desire. All manner of things then went well.

It is not too far a stretch to say that part of my being was shaped by my growing love for Suzanne and shaped in a way that brought our attitudes towards food and animals closer together. An ethically based vegetarianism, and the values and desires that the latter involves, have become something that we share. It is part of our *being together*, although I am now a vegan and our dietary tastes do not happen to be particularly close except in the values and the value-related desires they express. We eat different breakfast cereals and prefer different kinds of soya milk. I am a casserole person and like hearty stews while she has a fondness for salads. We join together in mutual admiration of vegan BLTs served on summer's days at Heaphy's cafe in Glastonbury but on few other points. We share our values and our desire to eat in a way that minimizes our connection to harm, but there is a strong element of distinctiveness in which our separateness is preserved. In countless large and small ways our desires have shifted into line with what the other wants and with what the other recognizes as important. On some matters, such as diet and animals, Suzanne has been my guide. On others, such as the merits of Wagner, olives and the unimportance of being conventional, she has come to embrace some of my enthusiasms. But in doing so, neither of us has become deferential to the other; our desires have shifted rather than being sacrificially subordinated to those of another person. This leads me to think there may be something true about the idea that love can shape autonomy rather than conflicting with it.

Mortality and loss

Barring separation, pacts and accidents, any shared life comes to an end with the death of one partner. Reflection on this may make the image of the conjoined lovers appear as a tantalizing but ultimately cruel fantasy. It may encourage the recognition of an ultimate separateness that stands in the way of any genuine togetherness. It may seem to show just how separate we humans are and must always remain.

When a partner or a lover or spouse dies, consoling truths about death may soften the blow. We are all part of a reality that exceeds us and is, in obvious ways, more important than any of us. Everything that we are must make way for, and may be taken up in, future life. Our bodily constituents are part of a larger cycle of life in which we are each, in turn, consumed and swallowed up by the earth. But even thoughts of this sort, infused with a sense of spirituality, or with hopeful longing for a more personal form of survival, will not protect us from grief upon the loss of a lover or soulmate.

In a more individualist and perhaps less life-embracing vein, we may think of our own death as something that only we can undergo, as something that is our ownmost limit and is in this respect akin to personal real-estate. This is a familiar and tempting line of thought. It may, after all, be nice for a time for any one of us to imagine that we have a composite or combined identity with someone else, but the harsh truth may be that this is not so. It is tempting to say that couples are simply chance combinations of separate individuals who do not always exercise or recognize their own autonomy. Thinking of oneself as part of a couple may then seem to involve turning away from the authentic nature of our own being. It is worth reflecting, in this context, that while the heroes of romantic literature in the eighteenth and nienteenth centuries were generally great lovers or were for the most part *paired off*, the major existentialist anti-heroes of twentieth-century literature were loners and, typically, men. Even when in bed with a woman their separateness was tangible. Even Nietzsche's allegorical *Thus Spoke Zarathustra*, not itself an existentialist text but a text that anticipates something of the atmosphere of existentialism, shows us an isolated individual who tells his would-be followers that both he and they must go and be alone (1986: 103). There seems to be a demanding honesty to this way of thinking. Perhaps we are not tempted to live quite such heroic lives but we can still admire them from a distance.

Against this temptingly individualist picture of human life I want to suggest that reflection on our own mortality, and on the mortality of those we love, may help to shed a more positive light on the imagery of joining. It may help us to understand the idea that two humans can genuinely (authentically) be connected in a deep and loving manner that shapes their very being and makes sense of the claim that they share a life. But in order to make this approach work I need to get beyond the observation that "We don't know what we've got 'til it's gone". Frequently we *are* complacent about the presence of those we love. We act as if there were an unlimited supply of time available to us: time enough to make all our feelings clear; time enough to enjoy the company of those we care about and to see everyone right at the end of the day. But what I want to suggest is that the loss of another, the process of bereavement and the grief it involves, discloses something *more* than this everyday complacency.

Consider the following rudimentary picture of bereavement. It is a tract of experience that is involuntary in the sense that we cannot choose to start or to stop it. To some extent, we must simply let it run its course. It involves a demotivating state and, for a lengthy period of time, we are in some respects inconsolable. Frequently, bereavement involves guilt and sometimes it involves anger. Always it involves grief and finally it involves a greater if temporary appreciation of our own mortality. At the risk of stating the obvious, the experience of bereavement is not so much unpleasant as dreadful. It takes us to a very dark place and we do not know how to return.

In this latter respect bereavement is akin to mental illness, although there is a normative contrast that may be drawn between the two, a contrast that we can make in terms of "ought" claims. Although bereavement and certain forms of mental illness may feel much the same, and although bereavement can get out of control and can lead into mental disorder, the two still play significantly different roles in a life. Bereavement can be a necessary part of a good human life in a way that mental illness cannot. For this reason it sometimes makes sense to say that for our own sake we *ought* to grieve but it makes no sense at all to say that for our own sake we *ought* to be mentally ill.

No doubt there are many other features of bereavement that we might want to acknowledge and they may help us to deepen the contrast. The above comments are intended only as a gloss and are far from exhaustive. What they can help us to do is focus on the connection between love, desire and one particular emotional component of the bereavement process: grief. To make sense of this emotion, I shall assume that emotions in general are not just raw twinges of an experienced but otherwise indescribable sort. Instead, they can be given complex descriptions. Whatever else grief involves (or at least the kind of grief that is part of bereavement), it involves a *belief* that someone happens to be dead. More cautiously, it involves something belief-like, something that we might call a "construal", a "seeing as" or a "perceptual experience that". Grief also involves intermittent physiological and psychological *feelings* such as feeling cold or numb, feeling that the world is a very dark place, experiencing a heightened sensitivity to our own bodily states and to otherwise unnoticed processes such as breathing. When it is the genuine item and not a faked-up or false emotion, grief of this sort also involves a *desire* that the deceased be alive and well again.

We can, of course, engage in all manner of arguments about whether these things are constitutive parts of the emotion of grief or whether they are its accompaniments. Given that it is difficult to make any sense of the idea that someone could genuinely be grief-stricken in the absence of *any* of the above, I shall take it that they are all partly constitutive of what grief involves. But while this is a complex description, I shall make no judgement about whether it is a description of a number of separate mental states or a description of one single unitary mental state about which a great deal may be said. Given this account of grief, the following two claims can now be advanced. First, the involuntariness of bereavement is partly a matter of the involuntariness of the grief it involves. And second, in so far as any one of us has a deeply rooted desire for the well-being of another person, we will be vulnerable to the experience of grief upon their loss and there will be nothing we can do to avoid it.

Steps can be taken to make matters slightly easier for ourselves when we are grief-stricken but nothing short of the discovery that it has all been a ghastly mistake will suddenly take the grief away. In this sense we are inconsolable. And part of the reason for our inconsolability is that absolutely nothing will work as a way of giving us what we want. The desire involved in grief plays a fundamental role in blocking our path. What we want when we are grief-stricken, what we *desire*, happens to be utterly unattainable. We want the other person back, and this is never going to happen. To be grief-stricken is *in this respect* to be in a dreadful predicament that we are helpless to end. Given this, we can begin to understand just why the overall process of bereavement is so demotivating and is akin to a form of entrapment. It removes our desire to act because action will not help and neither will anything else.

Understanding this can allow us to see love more clearly. It can allow us to see that our desires *bind us* to the other person. When we love someone, particularly when we love them in the sexualized intimate way that spouses or partners do, we have a defeasible reason to want what they want. But even more fundamentally, our own familiar and everyday desires, the desires that relate to our well-being, become *conditional* on their well-being.

It is an often unnoticed feature of almost any desire that it is liable to be conditional on something. If you want a new car, you will do so on the condition that you are still able to drive it when it arrives and that it is not, instead, part of some gruesome trade-off. When I want a vegan ice cream, I do so on the condition that I will still want it at the time when it is served. When a friend wants someone to play a particular tune, they do so on the condition that the speakers are not disconnected at the same time. Our desires are only satisfied if we get what we want under reasonable and acceptable conditions. A classic illustration of the point is the folk-tale scenario in which someone (let us say "Mr Johnson") meets the devil at the crossroads and is offered three wishes in return for his soul. The agreement is struck, but every time Mr Johnson gets what he has requested the circumstances are so ordered that his desire is not genuinely satisfied. He gets to be wealthy, but trapped in a cave; he gets to be free, but everyone else is dead; he has everyone brought back to life but now he is the one who is dying. Mr Johnson learns about the conditional nature of desires the hard way, and at considerable expense.

When we love someone, at least some of our desires become conditional on their well-being. Even the commonplace and everyday desires we have, such as the desire to visit a coffee shop every few days, or to watch a favourite television programme, or to celebrate at Yule and Christmas, can become conditional on our loved one being hale and hearty and there with us. Without their presence, or at least their well-being, the simple enjoyment of these things would no longer be the same. In many cases it would no longer be possible.

This is one of the ways in which love for the other is deep. It involves a desire for their well-being that works its way into the fibre of our own being, reshaping and meshing with the other desires it finds there. And while this may not amount to actual physiological merging, the comprehensive annihilation of individuality or the establishment of an undifferentiated "we", it is nonetheless a sharing and a joining-together of a very real sort. It is the kind of sharing and joining-together that helps us to makes sense of the dreadfulness of the separation that comes with death. It also helps to explain the anomalous respect in which the otherwise demotivating process of bereavement allows a *new* and destructive motivation to emerge: the motivation to end things, not so much out of a dislike for the dreadfulness of grief, but as a way of rejecting a world that goes on without our loved one or as the only way we can think of to "be with" them again *in at least some sense.*

Here, I might be accused of lapsing into romanticism, into the old idea of *liebestod*, the idea of making sense of intimacy and sex as a figurative or literal death. In my defence I shall point out the utterly unromantic implications of what I have claimed about grief and about joining together. Given that we *do* recover from grief (albeit to a greater or lesser degree) and that the process of bereavement *does* come to an end, there must be at least a partial and incomplete disentangling of our desires from the impossible desire to have the other person back again. Bereavement disrupts but it also prepares us for a return to the world, a world without the person we love.

This again sets it apart from mental illness, not just in the sense that the latter can go on and on but in the sense that bereavement plunges us into a darkness or void that we must go through in order to find a way to go on without the other person. This may be one of the reasons why bereavement so often involves guilt as well as grief. We may, in part, be guilty about our own survival but there is also a sense in which guilt tracks a real separation in which we may seem to be complicit. Caught up in bereavement's earlier stages, we may feel the almost impossible difficulty of being able to continue. In its latter stages we feel guilty about our ability to do so. We feel guilty about our steady return to the world. When we slowly emerge at the other end of the process, we begin to enjoy again the simple everyday pleasures that were, for a time, lost to us. And this is an indication that our desire for these things has ceased to be quite so conditional on the *well-being* and the presence of the person we have loved and lost. We may always, and for the rest of our lives, wish they were back with us once again, and we may feel that our life remains incomplete without them, but we can no longer love them *in quite the same way*. Our return to the world involves a partial and incomplete disentangling of our everyday desires from an impossible loving concern for their well-being. Our desires can increasingly, if only to some extent, be satisfied even in the permanent absence of the loved one. In this respect we become more independent, but it is an independence we are forced into, and an independence of a sort that may feel almost like betrayal.

Perhaps it is a fear of this process of readjustment and partial recovery, and not just the burden of going on, that drives some people to take their own lives just when we expect them to recover from grief. An ability to *come out at the other end* may be enough to place anyone's sense of the genuineness and continuity of their own love in doubt. But guilt of this sort results from the depth of a person's love rather than its absence.

6. Irreplaceability

Suppose a man says to a woman that she has "the most beautiful eyes in the world" and the woman says to the man that he is "wonderful in a way that nobody else is". Do we take these statements at face value? It would be odd to do so. The woman *might* rush off and compare her features and dimensions with photographs of various other women who exemplify and fix her standard for beauty. But it would be odd to suppose that the man is applying any precise standard at all, that he is even familiar with all the eyes in the world or that he is commenting *only* about her eyes rather than commenting about *who she is* and *what she means to him*. Utterances of this sort do not indicate that the speaker has set himself up as a judge of some extensive competition in which the rest of humanity are unwitting entrants. If asked, "Why are my eyes so beautiful?", he might reply, "because they are yours", and the obvious circularity here would reinforce the point that while he *is* commenting about her beauty, he is not engaging in a strict and literal description that is focused on precisely one aspect of her anatomy. It would similarly be odd for the man to puzzle about the true nature of his own wonderfulness in the light of her comments and to do so in order to gain personal insight. These are familiar ways of speaking, terms of endearment. They say something but they do not count as evidence for the pessimist's claim that love involves delusion in the form of an overestimation of those we love.

One thing that such comments do indicate is that the speaker sees the other person as special and *set apart* from everyone else.

Love, and especially so in the case of sexualized intimate love, involves this kind of individuation, this kind of *setting apart*. And it is tempting to make sense of it by appeal to the projection of beauty, intelligence and charm that no one else possesses, or at least beauty, intelligence and charm that nobody else possesses to the same degree. This would involve overestimation of a special sort that might secure loyalty and stand in the way of any "trading-up" to secure a better beloved, but it would still be based on delusion. Setting aside its convenience as an explanation, just why should we buy into this picture? Well, one reason to do so is that this pessimistic account of the nature of love does fit well with some aspects of our experience. Love is sometimes like this, at least in its initial stages, and particularly so when we fall in love for the first time. Everything in the world can then seem more vivid and lively. And it is true, as a point about experience, that sometimes when we love we *do* overestimate. But perhaps this is less common than we may imagine, or it may be restricted to particular occasions and episodes. It may apply more to *falling in love* than it does to the *loving* that comes afterwards.

I want to set out a picture of this ongoing process of loving that does justice to the idea of *setting apart* but does not require any appeal to the projection of fictional properties. At the very heart of this picture will be the requirement that we see those we love as irreplaceable. And whereas the pessimistic appeal to overestimation builds on the model of first loves and of falling in love, I shall build my understanding of irreplaceability on the experience of grief.

There is an obvious sense in which grief is bound up with our way of seeing. As already noted, this is partly a matter of desire. In grief, we desire to have someone back again and we also recognize the utter hopelessness of this desire. We see that the other is gone and will not return. What shapes this recognition of the hopelessness of our desire is an awareness that those we love are in some important sense unique. I am inclined to say that this is true in the case of *any* kind of love that deserves the name and that it helps us to mark off those occasions on which we may speak about "love" in a robust sense from those occasions on which we use it as a manner of speaking or as a synonym for "really liking". Some of us "love" a nice glass of wine and some of us "love" dark or raw chocolate but, so long as the vintage and batch are the same, one glass and one chocolate is as good as another and no better.

Intimate love is different from this fondness for consumable items in all sorts of ways. It grows or withers between lovers and makes us especially vulnerable to loss. Those who shy away from such vulnerability will have a difficult time coming to terms with love, a difficult time acknowledging and embracing their own true feelings. Otherwise-intelligent people have been known to do this: to hide in the face of love or to redescribe it into something that is safe and less threatening. A disturbing example of this can be found in a letter from the Roman philosopher Seneca. As a Stoic, he was committed to the view that virtue is *sufficient* to guarantee a good life and that the good man must therefore be invulnerable. In line with this, he tells a young correspondent not to despair or to lose his equanimity over the loss of a friend. After all, friendship may be a very good thing but new friends can always be found to replace the old ones:

> The wise man, nevertheless, unequalled though he is in his devotion to his friends, though regarding them as being no less important and frequently more important than his own self, will still consider what is valuable in life to be something wholly confined to his inner self. (1977: 52)

There are various tensions in this claim. A benevolent overestimation of friends sits cheek-by-jowl with a move that threatens to strip value away from all that exists outside of the self. A similar claim is applied by Seneca to family and children. He admires Stilbo, whose town was sacked and burned and whose entire family was lost in the conflagration but who nonetheless claimed that all his true valuables, his *just character*, had survived:

> We are impressed at the way some creatures pass right through fire without physical harm: how much more impressive is the way this man came through the burning and the bloodshed and the ruins uninjured and unscathed. Does it make you see how much easier it can be to conquer a whole people than to conquer a single man? (*Ibid.*: 52–3)

We may appreciate the concern here for the dignity of those who refuse to be utterly destroyed by grief and misfortune, a concern that indicates a real attachment to the plight of the individual in the midst of turmoil. But I also wonder about the kind of suffering and detachment from suffering that led Seneca to make his point in just this way, by appeal to "coming through the ruins uninjured and unscathed". Even if the letter is an attempt to explain a philosophical position about the consolations of virtue, the claim that Seneca makes is singularly unrealistic and lacking in its appreciation of human attachment. Resilience may be a good thing but those who fail to acknowledge and to accept the genuineness of their loss are not in a good, admirable or even healthy state of mind. At the core of Seneca's view of human relations is a reluctance to love anything other than a rarefied wisdom: a reluctance to accept our familiar vulnerability to loss.

A more curious, cautious and modern attempt to represent those we love as replaceable is set out by Derek Parfit in a thought experiment that involves physical duplication. The reader of Parfit's book *Reasons and Persons* (1984) is invited to imagine that their loved one steps into a teleporter and is then dismantled in order to capture all the information that is relevant to their physical state.

This fine-grained information is then transmitted to another tele-porter, which then assembles a duplicate. Effectively, the person you love is killed and replaced by someone who is physiologically and behaviourally identical, item for item and gesture for gesture. For the purposes of the experiment we may ignore the fact that there is prob-ably something wrong with the physics required for constructing teleportation equipment of this kind. (It would require a fine-grained determinability that our best science suggests is impossible.) But we might still imagine that exact duplication could result from extremely fortuitous luck, as a chance configuration of matter or from informed guesswork. Given this, we may ask the question that most concerns Parfit. If we loved the person who stepped in, should we also love the physiologically identical person who steps out? His intuition about this scenario is that we clearly and obviously *would* do so and *should* do so. "I fall in love with Mary Smith. How should I react after she has first used the Replicator? I claim both that I would and that I *ought* to love her Replica" (1992: 295).

The purpose of the exercise, from Parfit's point of view, is to try to support a bigger claim that the self is not what we imagine and not as important as we might imagine. In this respect, it contrasts markedly with Seneca's approach. For Parfit, the replacement of those we love by duplicates would be pretty much as good as their survival by ordinary means, and our own replacement by a dupli-cate would similarly be pretty much as good as our own ordinary survival as well. In other words, selves are not robust in some deep way that should lead us to worry about replacement. Even among fictional scenarios this is an unusual example of its kind. It is unsettling in a way that is rarely true of thought experiments. In some sense they are not at all like real ethical deliberation, but this experiment seems to challenge and confuse our understanding of a deep commitment. How could we refuse to recognize the claims of an exact replacement for the person we love? But doing so might involve something akin to betrayal.

This is a thought experiment that I have explained to students on a number of occasions. Mostly they reject Parfit's intuition but a small number are prepared to accept it. Perhaps this is an indication that I explain matters in a way that skews the results. My neutrality is, admittedly, paper thin. I flag up my own view quite openly, in the confident belief that it will not be universally shared and that the position will be challenged. The correct response to the problem (if there is one) is not, after all, obvious.

It may also be noted that Parfit's scenario does not strike at the idea that others are irreplaceable in *every* sense. In practice, when we lose someone we will never find another. Nobody else we encounter in life will ever be exactly the same. When we move outside the confines of thought experiments, and think about what life is actually like, we can readily accept that although we may meet some person who resembles the loved one we have lost, there will always be differences of face and gesture, attitude and tone of voice. Physiologically and behaviourally identical duplicates will not be available to us and so *in practice* our loved ones are utterly irreplaceable. Because of this, reflection on Parfit's thought experiment could not take the edge off grief, but it is not designed to do so. He is not suggesting that if our true love should go, we may sometimes find another who meets the same specifications.

But if Parfit is right about the idea that we would and should love duplicates *were they available*, then a particular kind of irreplaceability would be ruled out. While those we love would be, to all intents and purposes, *practically irreplaceable*, they would not be *irreplaceable in principle*. It would be conceivable (although not very realistic) that an identical copy of a loved one could become available and perhaps they would do just as well as the original. What I want to suggest is that this claim draws its plausibility from an appreciation of how psychologically compelling our longing for another can be, how difficult, almost impossibly difficult, it can be to let go and how difficult it can be to set aside our feelings for another. But ultimately Parfit's position also draws its plausibility from a mistaken way of picturing of love, and in particular from the mistaken view that love is a response to the attractive or distinctive physiological properties and behaviours that may be immediately present in our encounters with others.

The uniqueness of those we love

How could we, upon the loss of a loved one, not be overwhelmed by the appearance in our lives of someone who was indistinguishable from them, someone who acts in the same old way and who claims to recollect the same events? How could we fail to cherish such a being or remain unresponsive to their pleas? With Parfit, I am inclined to hold that it would be extremely difficult for us to do so, if only because of the difficulty involved in accepting that someone is truly gone. Upon the loss of another, we still expect them to walk through the door, and this is just what a duplicate would do, all the time looking and acting exactly like our loved one. We could not treat them just like a new arrival. After all, it takes time to come to terms with death and, at the danger of sounding a little reductionist, we are not wired in a way that allows us instantly to accept it. In the presence of a dead body we do not, for example, act in the way we do during subsequent visits to a burial site. If confronted by an identical replacement, it would be impossibly difficult to say, "You are not the one that I love", and simply to walk away.

Parfit's duplication scenario taps into this difficulty of accepting loss and the impossibility of doing so instantaneously, but it does so at the risk of oversimplifying the psychological predicament involved. There is, after all, something unnerving about the very idea of a physiologically exact duplicate: a residual suspicion that such a being would not be the genuine item but would be akin to a changeling. The unnerving and threatening character of doubling, duplication and the changeling are, after all, familiar cultural and literary motifs. The common emphasis of the narratives in which they figure is the dual response they induce: the special combination of attraction and repulsion.

Consider a slightly more enriched narrative than Parfit's thought experiment, but again a fictional narrative concerning duplication. Stanislaw Lem's *Solaris* (1961) is, to my mind, the most interesting book Lem ever wrote. A classic of the sci-fi genre, turned into a film successively by the Soviet director Andrei Tarkovsky and more recently by Steven Soderbergh, it is a psychological drama set mostly aboard a monitoring station that is situated above a strange, ocean-covered planet with peculiar mimetic features. In the more recent film version, the central character Chris Kelvin (played by George Clooney) arrives at the station and encounters a planetary surface that is fluid and changing but is not like any sea that we know. It has the capacity to mimic whatever it encounters and also the capacity to reach deeper into our thoughts and feelings to duplicate those we love but have lost. It can produce, for any of us, a copy of the person we happen to desire most whether it be a lost child, a lover or a spouse.

Kelvin arrives in a primed condition. He is recently bereaved and, like the others on the station, he is visited by one of these duplicates, a woman who seems, to all intents and purposes, to be his dead wife. There are, admittedly, some low-level physiological differences. The duplicates have a remarkable capacity for recovery from trauma, the soles of their feet are soft, like a child's, and there is also a noticeable behavioural difference: the duplicates cling. They find it impossibly difficult to tolerate distance and absence. They are beings whose embrace can seem to engulf and consume. On the one hand, there is attraction and the promise of a longing finally satisfied. On the other, there is repulsion. Something about these creatures is definitely threatening. As duplicates they are, in a sense, parasitic on the originals. Options for dealing with them include killing them, which doesn't work because the replacements are in turn replaced, and killing yourself, which in a sense does work but the duplicates continue to cling, emphasizing their changeling status and lack of true humanity.

The first of these visitors that Kelvin meets is tricked by him. He shoots her off into space. The second he comes to love, or at least he claims to. But in the book, unlike the film, his character claims to love her *for who she is now*, and not as the continuation of the woman he loved before. But are we to believe this? Perhaps and perhaps not. The fact that he loves her (if he does) is clearly related to the traits and properties she happens to have in common with his dead wife. Even if he loves her *now*, as the different woman she is, the genesis of this love is related to her duplication of someone else, someone with a prior claim on his affections. But does he really love her at all? In such a scenario, there would be robust grounds for the duplicate to be sceptical about being loved (another indication that scepticism about being loved is not always misplaced). Once informed of the full facts, the duplicate might reasonably suspect that the love of Kelvin is still for the earlier woman from whom her own template was formed.

Concerns drawn from Freud and Proust that not only is love shaped by the past, but that the past in question defines love's true objects, might seem, in this instance, to be well placed. In the *Solaris* example, *someone* is loved but just *who* this someone is may be unclear. On a generous account we may say that Kelvin loved his wife and that he now loves the duplicate. If the overall scenario were genuinely possible this could be the case. Awkwardly, it seems to return us to Parfit's idea that those we love are replaceable. But this appearance is deceptive. Using a familiar (but disputed) philosophical terminology of "reasons for love", we may say something of the following sort: Kelvin has reasons to love his wife and he has reasons to love the woman that he meets at the monitoring station but these reasons are not exactly the same. The most obvious reason he has for loving the duplicate is that she is a copy of the original, with all the feelings, fears and vulnerabilities that this entails (vulnerabilities made clear by the clinging and symbolized by the child-like feet). But this is *not* why he loves the original, who is not a copy of anything.

Lem's scenario points to the possibility that originals are not replaceable, but in some qualified sense, and for a limited period of time, duplicates may be. They may be replaceable at least prior to the point at which they have a significantly distinctive history of their own. While they love only because of a shared history that is not truly *theirs*, one duplicate will be pretty much as good as another. But it does not follow from this that one original would be pretty much as good as another. Beyond this, there is also a question about how quickly Kelvin could come to love the duplicate. Even if he had reasons to do so this might take time, and this again may make it difficult to think of his love as the same old love directed at a new replacement object.

Faced with intriguing scenarios of this sort, the minority of students who think that love would transfer over, more or less unproblematically, point towards physiological and behavioural identity and to the seemingly obvious fact that whatever properties draw us to love an original would also draw us to love the replacement. This assumes, as I also do, that we cannot appeal to a hidden-away, soul-thing that was inside body 1 (Kelvin's original wife) but not body 2 (the duplicate), or inside the body of the person who steps into one of Parfit's teleporters but not inside the body of the person who steps out. But if love is not a response to such a hidden-away entity then it may seem to make sense to say that it must be a response to, and *about*, the various physical or physiological qualities a person happens to possess, or about the behaviour with which these properties are correlated. And in every instance these are things that *can* be copied.

To make sense of love in this way is to embrace what is sometimes known as "the quality theory of love". It is (problematically) attributed to Plato, along with the suggestion that he does not allow for the love of whole persons but only for the love of the various lovable properties they happen to instantiate (beauty, goodness and virtues of various sorts). This is unfair in Plato's case. We may, after all and *up to a point*, distinguish between the human who is loved and the grounds on which they are loved. But the quality theory still has a widespread currency. Duplication and replacement scenarios such as Parfit's thought experiment play on it as if it were the only plausible way of picturing love.

But it is a misleading picture. It discounts, or fails to give due credit to, something that talk about love as a response to the *inner self*, or to the *soul* of another, happens to capture very well, albeit in a roundabout way. What it captures is the fact that there is always something important that is not *immediately present* in any actual encounter with another human being, and arguably the same applies to encounters with creatures of any other sort. There is always something we do not and cannot see simply by looking at or becoming familiar with their body. Because of this, the idea of a soul-thing latches on to a real feature of experience. However, this special something need not be understood as an immaterial essence that is separate from all that is physical. What cannot be seen simply by looking at a body may instead be understood as the relational properties of the other person, and in particular their relation to a unique past. In philosophical jargon we might say that each individual has a "unique causal history" that no duplicate could ever have. A duplicate could, of course, have all sorts of information about the past and copies of someone's memories, but when they believed themselves to be remembering they would not be doing so. A duplicate could not *genuinely* remember the past because they were not there.

In matters of love, the past is important. So, for example, I do not want to go home to a physiologically exact duplicate of Suzanne, freshly assembled by one of Parfit's teleportation devices or put together by the sea of Solaris. I want to go home to the same Suzanne that I met at the end of my teens and who sat out with me under the stars. I want to be with *this* particular and unique being who has a history that no other being could have, a history that at least in part binds us together. She is not only *in practice* irreplaceable because it just so happens that nobody is like her, but also *in principle* irreplaceable. A duplicate could, of course, be made or might spring into existence as an unlikely chance configuration of matter, and such a duplicate might have all sorts of false memories, enough even to fool me if I did not know about the switch. But a duplicate could never have exactly the same history as the original. Because of this, I could not have the same shared history with it (or her) and neither of us could have the same reasons for love.

This does not commit me to a denial that some features of the past of two persons can be similar and even correlated in various ways that might give a third person reasons to love them both. Some (but not all) of these reasons might even be the same. Perhaps this can be seen more clearly in the case of parental love rather than sexualized intimate love. Both the loved individuals might be children of a single parent. This fact would give the parent a similar reason to love them both *but not as replacements for each other.* And they would still be unique individuals by virtue of the distinctive and irreproducible features of their personal histories. Having a past that is similar, even in important respects, is not the same as actual duplication and, consequently, it does not offer any possibility of replacement without loss.

To some extent our concern for the past carries over to non-animate objects as well. Directly behind me, sitting beneath the window and looking more elegant than I will ever manage, there is a wind-up gramophone from the 1920s or 1930s. Neither my wife nor myself have ever figured out which date is closest. Suzanne travelled to Edinburgh to buy the gramophone as a Christmas present more than a decade ago. She travelled through the rain, the cold and the snow, as well as arranging covert and ill-advised meetings with men in cafes in order to get the needles and some good original records. In retrospect, enquiring about needles in a major city may have been open to misinterpretation. Be that as it may, nothing sounds quite like Caruso singing *Pagliacci* on the wind-up. This object is tied in to part of our early history together. An indistinguishable and mechanically identical machine would just not be the same because part of our care for it is care about this history. Although here, what looks like a parallel case may turn out to be simply an extension of love for an irreplaceable person. At least part of my reason for attachment to the gramophone is my love for Suzanne: for the particular, unique and *in principle* irreplaceable woman who brought this item into our lives.

To reinforce the point, what makes each of us unique and beyond any possibility of full duplication is our past and *not* our physiology or associated behaviour. The same goes for the uniqueness of those we love. Appearances change. We grow, age and may lose whatever attractions we once had. But love that is love need not be dislodged by this process. Nor do we need to fall in love anew with a succession of individuals who constitute some overall serial person. Love is capable of a constancy that is sensitive to humans as changing and growing beings; it is a response to a unique individual who ages with us over time. Shakespeare's familiar sonnet on this theme expresses matters more beautifully that I could ever manage:

> … Love is not love
> Which alters when it alteration finds,
> Or bends with the remover to remove.
> O no, it is an ever fixèd mark
> That looks on tempests and is never shaken;
> It is the star to every wand'ring barque,

> Whose worth's unknown although his height be taken.
> Love's not time's fool, though rosy lips and cheeks
> Within his bending sickle's compass come;
> Love alters not with his brief hours and weeks,
> But bears it out even to the edge of doom.
>   If this be error and upon me proved,
>   I never writ, nor no man ever loved.   (Sonnet 116)

Of course, this is not intended as a detailed analysis of love and it is not strictly true on all points. People fall out of love all the time without it being the case that they were never truly in love. Love, although once genuine, can be lost or ended or deliberately eroded when we find that it is damaging. A relationship and the love that is part of it may succumb to the tempests or to the ups and downs of a shared life. People may find that they have drifted apart over time without even noticing it. We may, sometimes with good reason, doubt the constancy of our love for another or doubt that we are loved precisely *because* love gained is not necessarily love secured for all time. Love can alter when it finds alteration. One partner may lose sexual interest in another, and love may then be placed in question, not just because of the annoying absence of sex but because of the absence of all sorts of intimacy that go with sex. Alternatively, we may think of extreme cases of physical alteration such as the onset of advanced dementia. Alterations of this sort destroy a being's identity. Sometimes they lead to a routine care that replaces intimate love and finally replaces love of any kind. It can become impossibly difficult to associate the shell of the human that remains with the vibrant being with whom we once shared a life. We may then continue to love someone but not to associate them with the tangible human body that we can see and watch and feel for.

Nonetheless, love can and often does survive the rather different alterations that Shakespeare has in mind: the alterations that go together with the processes of sharing time, ageing together, and building a common history. Perhaps we might then say that love involves valuing a relationship, and if this does not exclude or trump or overshadow the valuing of the other person it may be harmless to make this claim (Kolodny 2003). Another way of making the point would be to say that a relationship gives reasons for love or (more guardedly) that it enables other considerations to operate as reasons for love.

Whatever formulation we use to make sense of the pivotal role played by the sharing of a relationship or, in other terms, the sharing of a history, we may still be able to recognize both the weakness of duplication scenarios that take no note of the past, and the dependence on the "quality theory" of familiar forms of pessimism about the nature of love. Pessimism is *often*, perhaps *usually*, dependent on claims about the projection of imagined properties (or "qualities") on which love is supposedly based: the imagined properties that, in our beguiled eyes, belong to our beloved and set them apart from all others. More strongly, its plausibility depends *in all cases* on an appeal to such delusions, even if the appeal is hidden away in the background. But once uniqueness is understood in terms of the possession of a unique history there is no longer any need to assume that love makes those we love *seem* unique by projecting special properties onto them. We may still recognize their uniqueness without any such deluding act of projection. What then remains is only a reason to be cautious with regard to claims of love that are made in particular cases: claims about our loving others and about their loving us.

Knowing that we are loved

There is a special problem associated with a carefully hidden and unrequited love that is never betrayed by word or by deed. Should someone love us in this way, we might never be able to tell. And this reinforces the idea that knowledge about being loved may not be accessible or straightforward. It may even seem rather a mystery that any of us know that we are loved and loved in a genuine and deep way, a way that does not depend on our looks and our transitory attractions but on our being who we are. Just how do we *know* that we are seen and cared for as unique and irreplaceable? There is room here for doubt. We can doubt love's extent, depth and ultimately its genuineness. Such a personal and unsettling scepticism cannot be removed simply by discrediting pessimism about the nature of love. After all, others might bask in the enjoyment of a full, genuine and non-delusional love but the supposed love that another has for us might lack these desirable features. Genuine love may have its false imitations. And in some respects, an acceptance that love enjoyed by others *can* be wonderful may add to our unease. An awareness that something better is possible can make mere companionship seem second-rate, which, in a sense, it is.

Scepticism about the genuineness of someone's love for us, about truly being loved, is not exclusively or primarily a fear about deliberate and bloody-minded deception. There is, after all, nothing that will protect us from a calculating and cunning deceiver. Most of us accept this danger but hold that the likelihood of being deceived in this way is remote. Unless we are possessed of fame and fortune, the chances of anyone bothering to trick us systematically over a prolonged period of time are so slight that it is not, in most instances, worth worrying about. The pay-off would be far too low.

Worries about the genuineness of being loved do not require a special or unusual pathology. A routine scepticism about being loved can tap into ordinary insecurities that reach deeply into our past but not necessarily all the way back. As teenagers we come to doubt a great many things, and one of them is our ability to find someone who will love us and who will be loved by us in return. Unlike various other doubts that do, in most cases, eventually go away (such as "Will I ever have sex?") this doubt about securing love, and about loving, can persist and may become entrenched. A history of failed relationships, botched love affairs and connections to attractive others that do not quite get off the ground may convince us that we are right to be sceptical when faced with the latest person who claims that we are what they want, need and love. There is always the possibility that such scepticism is well founded and occasions on which claims of love are not malevolent or duplicitous but are nonetheless false.

In the face of this problem, it is tempting to appeal simply to faith and to trust in the other person. And no doubt faith and trust can be beautiful and, sometimes, both important and well placed. No doubt they are requirements if a loving relationship is to work. But perhaps we can say a little more. What I want to suggest is that scepticism about being loved is in some respects akin to philosophical scepticism about other minds. The latter turns on questions such as "How do we know that others are not just automata?" It seems that we have access to our own thoughts but lack access to the thoughts of others. Given this, perhaps others simply have no thoughts. Perhaps they are all behaviour and nothing else. Stated baldly in these terms, scepticism about other minds sets up an intriguing philosophical puzzle that is remote from everyday life. We are not fooled by the puzzle into genuine doubt. We are aware from the outset that other humans have minds just as we do. But still the puzzle remains.

It becomes a little less puzzle-like, and more of a problem, in the case of animals, because we do not know quite what it is like to experience the world as they experience it. And some individuals also take the other-minds problem seriously in the case of artificial intelligence. They suspect that computers might be able to think. But my interest here is not in drawing up a point-by-point comparison between scepticism about being loved and scepticism of this other sort. I simply want to draw attention to a shared background assumption. Scepticism about other minds, and the very idea that there *is* a problem about other minds, is based on a persuasive assumption that we know our own minds better than we know those of others *because* as far as knowledge by direct acquaintance goes, we do not know the minds of others at all.

This same assumption helps to drive scepticism about being loved. It seems to be the case that "I know my own feelings but I'm only guessing about how they feel". However, I want to suggest that, in the case of love and the emotions generally, this assumption is mistaken. It is simply not true to say that we are *automatically* the best judges of our own emotions and ultimately the best judges of whether or not we are in love. It is a feature of our emotions in general, and love in particular, that we can be wrong about them. We can be angry with someone but still refuse to accept that we are angry; we can resent someone but believe that we wish them well; and we can be jealous but stubbornly refuse to admit that this is how we truly feel.

A capacity for mistaken self-appraisal is something we readily recognize in the case of children. Let us suppose that your eight-year-old rushes into the house and, mimicking a recent television programme, announces that they are madly in love with the girl over the fence and that, although they have only just met her, they will love her forever and ever. Theirs apparently is a love that will last 'til the end of time (which is nice). They may also have made some very provisional plans to marry. The best policy may be to let the episode blow over. The child is not lying. They are not trying to deceive. Still less is there an imminent danger of their future life being suddenly mapped out. They are simply mistaken about being in love. And this is something that we may be fairly confident about.

We can be confident because we know that they lack a suitable frame of reference that would allow them, in some clear and practical manner, to understand what it is like to be in love in the relevant way. This is not to say that they have an incomplete or imperfect theory of love, or any theory at all. Most people have no such theory, and children especially so. What they lack is a history, and even the beginnings of a history, of deep erotic attachment to anyone outside their family circle. What they have access to, in the absence of such a history of attachment, is the experience of familial attachment together with access to an impressive and shared vocabulary. But whatever the child subsequently learns as the years roll by, it will never be enough to avoid the *possibility* of being mistaken about who they love, and the way in which they love them. In their teens they may find it difficult to accept that they love their parents in any sense. And even against the backdrop of a far greater experience of love, including sexualized intimate love, when they *begin* to fall in love with a friend or with a new acquaintance, they may be the last to know. Others may be aware of their predicament before either of the parties to an emerging love is fully aware of what has happened.

My point here is that the asymmetrical picture of being certain about our own feelings, but uncertain about the feelings of those who claim to love us, is a misleading picture. And while it might be argued that there is no asymmetry because we are equally uncertain about both, there are cases of *knowing that we love* and *knowing that we are loved* in which this does not ring true. We may not be infallible or uniquely authoritative about our emotions in general, and love in particular, but there is no deep problem of "scepticism about loving". Nor is the recognition of genuine love or of its absence always beyond our discernment. Consider the case from Joyce mentioned in the opening chapter: the episode from Joyce's short story "The Dead". Gabriel, who has been acting the part of the tolerant and well-established gent, doing his duty as the centrepiece of a party held by his aunts, suddenly finds out that while he has been assuming that all was well, and thinking for years with a fondness about his life with his wife Gretta, she has been harbouring a longing for a young man who was killed years earlier. What helps to make the revelation hit home is the recognition that, all along, there must have been a thousand indications that she was acting not out of love but out of a sense of duty and propriety. What makes Gabriel feel shame is not just the circumstance that he may not be loved as he imagined, but the sudden recognition of his own complacency and inability to see some of the things that must have been there all along, staring him in the face. He is the pitiable fellow glimpsed in the mirror, the man who cannot tell the difference between being loved and being tolerated.

It is the exceptional nature of Joyce's picture that makes us feel sympathy for Gabriel even though Gretta's life has been much harder. Although the possibility of error is always there, most of the time we know when we love someone, although coming to know that we love them can be more complicated and error strewn. In a stable and lasting love, innumerable hints, clues and indications guide our judgement about whether or not we love. And, just as it takes real effort to conceal the absence of love, so too it takes great effort to conceal its presence. This applies in our own case and also in the case of those who love us. For this reason, the genuineness of someone's love can, over time, be seen.

The hints, clues and indications that lead us to decide that we are genuinely in love are not so different from the hints, clues and indications that may lead us to accept that we are genuinely loved. In both cases, we need faith and trust, but the faith and trust is only in part a matter of faith and trust in the other person. It is also a matter of faith and trust in our own good judgement and in our ability to see clearly and to make sense of events, our ability to do what Gabriel so conspicuously failed to do. When it comes to the discernment of love, we need not be blind; we all have a good deal to go on. And this is particularly so in cases where we enjoy a signif-icant shared history with the other person, a history that allows us to make sense of our own emotional responses and theirs as well. Under such circumstances, unless we are pathologically uncertain, we can, over time, come to *see* that we are loved or that love is absent. More formally, when matters go well, we can make a well-founded judgement that we are loved and loved more or less as we would wish to be loved, for the unique individuals that we are. A long familiarity with the other person may also, and less reassuringly, lead us to the equally well-founded judgement that we are a convenient proxy for someone else, a stand-in for a now unattainable love. It may also allow us to pick up on and recognize those unwelcome changes that mark the end of love. We may see that the other person is merely going through the motions, that they no longer have any particular desire to be with us. Their interest in our day may have become negligible and other matters may have come to monopolize their attention and concern.

As a result of a shared history we may even, from time to time, come to know someone in ways that they do not know themselves. We may recognize the end of their love before they do, and they too may read us well, and in advance of our own awareness of love's end. For better or worse, our most reliable judgements about ourselves and about another person, about what each of us genuinely cares for and truly loves, may emerge out of a shared history in which neither party has privileged access to the truth. Neither has privileged access because the truth about love is not locked away in the privacy of our own hearts.

7. What can we love?

When we love someone in the intimate and sexualized sense, we value them in a special way. There may still be room for apartness, solitude and quiet contemplation (as much room as other commitments will allow) but generally we want to be with that person and we want to share things with them: activities, laughter, sex, time. We see them in the light of *our own* past as well as in the light of what we know about *their* past and, above all, we see them as unique and irreplaceable. They are beings whose loss would cause us to grieve and, at least in part, our grief when faced with their actual loss results from the fact that the everyday desires and concerns that we have for *our own* well-being have become entangled with our desires and concern for *their* well-being; the one has become bound up with the other. This is what sharing a life with someone is like. The prospect of never seeing them again, never being close to them again, is truly dreadful. It is awful in ways that go beyond even the awfulness of the loss of our own life.

Although love of this sort, and love in general, leaves us vulnerable to loss, I have nevertheless suggested (and to some extent argued) that it is a basic human need. We *need* to love and to be loved if we are to live well. And because of this, we need to be open to the possibility of loving others and accepting of their love. Openness to love is a key human virtue. A life without love would fall dreadfully short. I have also suggested that we need not be unduly disturbed by familiar forms of doubt about love, and particularly about sexualized intimate love. And I have claimed that love of this sort is a good exemplar of what love of any sort has to involve. That is to say, love in general may be seen more clearly once we understand sexualized love, although our understanding of any kind of love may only ever be partial and incomplete. We may only ever be entitled to say "up to a point" and "to some extent".

As well as being in some ways characteristic, sexualized intimate love is also in some ways unique and distinctive. But there are several reasons why I have taken it as a good *way in* to an overall understanding of love. One reason is that such love is essential for a good life in a way that is particularly clear. Unless we are in the grip of a theory, or have suffered from successive disappointments, or are plagued by a recurring scepticism about being loved, we *know* that it is good to love and to be loved in this way. More forcefully, we know that love of this sort is essential to our well-being.

Another reason for my focus on sexualized intimate love is that loving in any sense has to involve desire and that which is sexual exemplifies desire. But I have also focused on love of this sort for more personal reasons. It is sometimes remarked, as a paraphrase of Nietzsche, that philosophers are always engaged in autobiography. While I am not wholeheartedly committed to this view in all cases, it does, in some respects, apply here. While friendships have come and gone, grown weak and grown strong again, it is the love that I share with Suzanne, and hope to go on sharing with her, that has taught me most of what I know about love. It has taught me more than I have learned from Plato and Freud, more than I can say or explain. It has contributed more than anything else to my contentment and, I trust, also to hers. Had I chosen, instead, to concentrate on parental love, I would have been writing about a subject with which I am less familiar. I accept that parental love involves conditional desires of a sort that make a parent's well-being dependent on the well-being of their child or children. It can be deep and complicated and life enhancing. I know what it is like to be loved in this way, to be cared for and to be cherished by parents, and I can understand why Christians regard parental love as exemplary. But, like a growing number of couples, Suzanne and I have no children and this does *not* stand in the way of our contentment. Children may be a great blessing, a challenge and a source of joy, but I do not regard child-rearing and the love that it shapes as in any general sense necessary for a good human life. Perhaps some people cannot live well without raising children, but they are people of a different sort from me.

Had I chosen, instead, to write about the love of neighbours, as it is spoken of in the Bible and also to some extent in the Torah, I would have been attempting to write about something that I occasionally see in others but do not see in myself. I do not think that love of this sort has ever formed a part of my own life experience, either as a giver or as a recipient. It would be ungenerous to deny the possibility of loving and being loved in this way. Others, although perhaps fewer than we might imagine, seem to feel it. But this is love that may involve a specialized religious commitment that I do not share and that, again, I do not regard as in any way necessary if a life is to go well.

It is, instead, an understanding of sexualized intimate love, seen against the backdrop of our vulnerability to loss and grief, that shapes my understanding of love's connection to well-being, just as it shapes my understanding of the bounds of love and my answer to the question "What can we love?" As a response to this deceptively simple query, I propose a surprisingly simple reply: "We can love anything that we can grieve over". One obvious challenge to this claim draws on the fact that we can love some or other god who cannot die. But even in this context there is the possibility of grief and loss, albeit the grief and loss that goes with disillusionment on the part of the devotee. For some individuals, the loss of a belief in their god is like a death in the family. For others, it is less of a blow because their previous attitude was one of belief or fascination but never love. A point to note here is that "grief", as I shall use it from now onwards, is to be understood in a sense that does not tie it to the recognition of the death of some actual being, although it is always informed by our grasp of what the latter can be like.

Even in the absence of further counter-examples it may still seem slightly unusual or idiosyncratic to understand the bounds of what we can love in just this way, by appeal to the possibility of grief. It may seem unusual for two reasons. The first is that any kind of love for persons involves a desire for the other person's well-being. If we have no such desire then we do not love them. In line with this, it is tempting to generalize and to say, "We can love anything that can live well or be harmed". A more appealing way to reformulate this same point would be to say, "We can love anything that can flourish", or at least, "We can love anything that *we believe* is capable of flourishing". This could extend the bounds of love to other humans, animals and perhaps also various non-sentient but life-rich entities such as ancient woodland, eco-systems, bio-diverse environments and, in brief, *other living things.*

Against this it may be pointed out that some things can live well or flourish but we cannot obviously love or grieve over them. One candidate would be future generations or at least *distant* future generations. We do not stand in the right relation to them for grief to be a possibility. It is far from obvious that our contentment and our everyday concern for our own well-being could ever come to depend on their well-being. Yet they may, at some future time, flourish, and the idea that we can love anything that can flourish would seem to imply, counter-intuitively that we can love them. Less controversially, it may be recognized that we have obligations towards them. But the recognition of such obligations need not be constitutive of love.

If this appeal to future generations is not a persuasive reason to separate out love from the possibility of flourishing, we may instead shift our attention in another direction. There may be entities that are utterly bereft of life and perhaps we could care for them too in a special and deep way that might well be said to involve love. In search of a lifeless place, and at the expense of being a little speculative, let us go off-world and consider one of the other planets in our solar system, Mars for example. The terrain is remarkable, awe-inspiring, and we may still hope that it has subterranean life. But perhaps it is truly bereft of life. And if this is the case there would be nothing that, in any obvious sense, would count as the planet's flourishing (at least until we add some life forms). Faced with this consideration we could, perhaps, try to adopt a strained account of what flourishing involves so that it is achievable in the case of lifeless and stable entities. But this seems like an option of the last resort.

In spite of its barrenness, there is something wonderful about the planet *as it is*, with its many and remarkable mountains, the largest (albeit extinct or dormant) volcano in the solar system and a massive canyon that the Grand Canyon on Earth could fit into several times over. We could well imagine someone spending time in an artificial habitat on this strange world, coming to cherish it as the unique place it is, and doing so in a deep way that makes their own future contentment conditional on what is done to the planet. While it would remain difficult to make sense of the idea that such a lifeless place could flourish, a well-situated individual might readily make sense of the idea that it may be harmed or damaged in serious and objectionable ways. They could believe the planet would be damaged beyond repair if subjected to extensive mining, or ruined if it were landscaped into a peculiar suburbia for Earth's ever-growing population. Should they hold such a view, and hold that such destruction had actually occurred on an extensive scale, something akin to a grieving process could take place. We might then find it difficult to understand or describe their experience without drawing some comparison with grief upon the loss of another human.

It is difficult to see why we should then refuse to regard such a response as a genuine instance of grief. There could be a real sense of loss that could be deeply personal and that might not be assuaged by any prospect of possible restoration. A restored terrain, even one that might look exactly like the original, would be natural (given that the human restorers would themselves be natural agents) but it would have a quite different history from the previously existing and irreplaceable terrain that was formed long ago by inconceivably powerful impacts and by ancient, awe-inspiring geological processes. It might be denied that any human could truly grieve in this way for something so lifeless, but this is a claim about human psychology that I am happy to dispute. And should we accept that the sense of loss upon the apparent destruction of such a landscape could involve real grief, it will then be tempting to regard it as symptomatic or indicative of a special kind of love. In this context, and perhaps others, it makes sense to understand love in relation to the possibility of loss and grief rather than primarily understanding it in relation to a desire for flourishing or, more simply, well-being. Such a desire marks out our love only for living things and for humans in particular.

There is a second reason why it may seem surprising to say, "We can love anything that we can grieve over". Given the complexity and elusiveness of love, it may sound odd to sum matters up so briefly. However, there is an obvious sense in which my claim about love and grief shifts our enquiry rather than bringing it to a conclusion. To make some sense of love's limits and bounds we may have to ask all sorts of questions about grief. And this promises to be an enquiry that is by no means simple or straightforward. After all, not everything that looks like grief is the genuine item. Nor is the apparent absence of grief always indicative of the true state of affairs. Many things may disguise themselves as grief, and grief itself may take on a difficult-to-recognize form.

We may, for example, grieve but fail to see or to accept that we are grieving. A person could harbour a sense of resentment towards a dead parent but refuse to accept that they feel grief over their loss. Alternatively, someone might be in the grip of a theory about resilience and about the avoidability or the brevity of grief. They could then find it difficult to accept that their own inconveniently enduring state is one of grief rather than distress or anxiety of some other kind. In the case of grief, as with other emotions, there may be mistaken self-appraisals and self-deception. Nonetheless, the person who denies their grief can still be grief-stricken, while someone else who sincerely claims to be grief-stricken may be mistaken. Because of this, it can be difficult to track back from genuine grief to genuine love.

What I shall call "false grief" is a conspicuous feature of our world (Milligan 2008: 215–17). I shall suggest that it was present during the great public outpourings of emotion at the time of the death of Princess Diana and again in the immediate aftermath of the death of Pope John Paul II. While there were a great many *genuinely* grief-stricken individuals on both occasions, at least some of those who joined the crowds, and who watched the television in rapt attention, were caught up in a wave of public emotion that they did not truly share. They (or rather "we", because I experienced the same thing too) may have felt sorry for the deceased and they (again, "we") may have believed in the authenticity of their own apparent and short-lived grief. But *in at least some instances* what was felt was other than it seemed. And the fact that it did *seem* like real grief is crucial to my point. I am not concerned here with mere pretence. I am sympathetic to the view that false grief expresses something, such as a need or desire that may have little or nothing to do with the deceased. Such a need or desire, in the case of grief over the death of Pope John Paul, might be regarded as some kind of spiritual longing. And in this sense there may have been something valid or genuine about it.

Even so, my main reason for saying that *in at least some instances* the apparent grief was false grief is that, however intense, it did not emerge out of any history of caring or out of any sudden recognition of a history of reasons for caring. As an extreme case, we may think of lifelong atheists who happened to be on tour in Rome at the time of Pope John Paul's death and who found themselves caught up in the moving drama of the moment but who did not find their views about religion, or about John Paul's political leanings, in any way challenged. Alternatively, we might think of the apparent grief of long-standing republicans over the death of Diana, individuals with no special or personal connection to her, who were, again, caught up in the moment. At least some of the mourners on both occasions did not have the deeply rooted desires that it takes to be genuinely grief-stricken, desires that relate directly to the deceased. Whatever it was they were hoping for, whatever it was they desired, they did not have a desperate, futile longing to have their loved-one back again. A desire for the well-being of the deceased, or at least the wish that they had not been harmed, was not deeply entangled with their everyday desires for their own well-being.

Even so, there are various qualifications that may need to be added to this account of false grief. We may, and should, allow for displacement and accept that what counts as false grief for one individual can be genuine grief for another. And to say this is just to accept one of the ways in which we can be fooled by our own emotions and fooled also by their false counterparts. In the light of this, it may also seem tempting to say that, whatever we *seem* to be grieving over, our real grief always turns out to concern humans. Given my claim that the bounds of love are equal to the bounds of grief, such a view would entail that humans are also, always, the true object of our love. Apparent love for anything else would then turn out to be deceptive or false.

Love for animals

Against such a restriction of the bounds of love, I want to assert that we *can* and often *do* grieve for and love non-humans. And we love them in a way that may be illuminated by our understanding of sexualized intimate love. There is a sense in which we can come to share a life with animals, particularly so with cats, dogs and other creatures that we interact with in complex and significant ways. We can and often do regard them as unique and as irreplaceable beings even though we may, at a succession of times, share our lives with a succession of different creatures.

As an illustration of the point let us suppose that you have a pet cat and that it is killed on the road. You rush it off to the local replicator and have the cat cloned. Admittedly, the technology involved is currently beyond us, but let us suppose that one day it may be available and that before too long you are given a living duplicate. There are some people who would regard this as a good thing. Others would not do so for the obvious reason that the replacement would not *be* the original. It would lack the same history and you too would lack the same history of reasons for caring about it. Those who have a practical grasp of this may be said to understand what it is to regard pets as unique. They understand what it is to have a pet in an enriched sense that involves viewing them as irreplaceable, and in some respects dependent, companions.

An understanding of uniqueness and of the irreplaceability of these dependent companions can be shown in other ways too. We can see it at work in end-of-life decisions, when owners (alternatively "animal guardians") know that it is time to say goodbye because of the animal's suffering. Under such circumstances, the owner may sometimes know something that the vet does not. But what they know is not always linked to any ability to spot a physiological quirk that the vet might fail to notice. Instead, they are in a position to see the animal in the light of its unique, individuating, history. And this can give them a special kind of insight because it is a history that they are best placed to understand. For example, let us suppose that two dogs are suffering from pain in identical ways but the case for ending the life of either is not clear-cut. A little pain is not enough to warrant such a decision irrespective of whether we consider the case of humans or the case of animals of any other sort. Let us simply say that the legs of the dogs will no longer support them without at least some discomfort and that the discomfort is estimated as being much the same in both cases. Let us also suppose that the dogs have the same owner and that the latter knows that one dog was mistreated for years by a previous owner while the other was cared for. What range of considerations should now be included in the end-of-life deliberation?

Here, I want to suggest that it would be perfectly reasonable for the owner to consider the past of each animal and, in the light of their differing individual histories, to regard the pain and suffering involved in these cases as playing a significantly different life role. In one case it would amount to the *re-emergence* of suffering but in the other it would not. Looking at matters in this way again involves a response to both creatures as individual, distinctive and valuable beings for whom grief is possible. Seeing a companion animal in this way *can*, of course, be accompanied by overestimation and by the delusion that "He understands every word I say". But, as in the case of sexualized intimate love, it does not *require* such overestimation and it involves a way of seeing that makes grief not only possible but likely.

There is a large literature dealing with the symptoms of grief over the loss of companion animals: anger, guilt, loss of sleep and appetite, loss of motivation and a withdrawal from others. Such a condition can continue for months and a sadness and longing can remain in place long afterwards. But, again, we may wonder about whether such grief is genuine or false. We may be inclined to suspect that the death of an animal merely provides a trigger for something else. The possibility is not unreasonable. Consider a simple scenario in which a young woman inherits a dog from her recently deceased mother after the latter has died unexpectedly and alone. Let us suppose that the young woman works nearby, goes home every lunchtime to check on the dog and that whenever the dog does not respond immediately to her calls she experiences a rush of anxiety. There is a recurring worry: "Has something happened?" Now suppose this continues for months, during which she grows very fond of the dog, but all too soon it dies of old age. She grieves, but in this scenario there may at least be a question about who the grief is for (Margolies 1999: 298).

Similarly, let us imagine a young boy who is raised by his father and is told how unmanly it is to show emotions or to shed tears. Communication about feelings is not regarded as a strong point. Eventually the father dies and the boy, now a young man, tries to keep busy and to get on with things. Pretty soon everything settles down. Years later, he takes in a stray dog and comes to care for it. After a long time the dog dies, but during its final months it requires close attention and a good deal of affection. After its death the man grieves terribly. Through caring for the dog he has learned how to grieve. But again we may ask, "Just who is the grief for?" It is tempting to say that *in part* he is grieving for the loss of his father. But why should the story end there? Why can the grief not be *both* for his father and for the dog (Pitcher 1996: 118)? What may tempt us to go astray, and to regard his grief for the animal as merely apparent, is a mistaken view of grief: a failure to recognize its mixed intentionality or "aboutness". Any new grief may echo or recapitulate all those that have gone before. And this is what grief is usually like.

If we accept that the grief for the dog is genuine in either of these cases we shall have no good reason to question the genuineness of the owner's love for the animal or to regard it as second-rate. And in so far as we are prepared to allow that animals too can grieve for the loss of their companions (a phenomenon for which there is ample evidence) we should accept that our love for them need not be unreciprocated. Animals that can grieve can also, in some sense, love, although they may be at least as likely to love each other as they are to love humans. Be that as it may, the desire for such love from a companion animal does not have to be regarded as "needy" or neurotic. It may involve a desire for a real connection with another creature, a connection of a deep and life-enriching sort. In this sense of "getting beyond the ego" and "connecting with other beings", a human desire for transcendence is both real and familiar.

There are, of course, *some* limitations to a companion animal's ability to reciprocate. There are complex desires that even cats and dogs cannot share with us because the desires in question are too cognitively demanding. Some desires are also beyond other creatures in the same way that complex mathematics is beyond them, and for much the same reason. (Similarly, some desires are beyond humans.) But *in some sense* the contentment of a companion animal can still become tied to the well-being of a human or of another animal. There are complex issues here and it may not be entirely correct to say, "They can desire their own happiness and such a desire may become entangled with their desire for the well-being of another creature". However, it is not *entirely* misleading to state matters in this way and cautious reformulation could perhaps bring us closer to the truth. A further limitation is that companion animals cannot, in *every* sense, regard us as irreplaceable. They cannot, for example, regard us as "irrreplaceable even by a physiological duplicate" because of the linguistic and conceptual demands that this involves. Nonetheless, it seems excessively restrictive to rule out the genuineness of their love on these grounds alone, particularly when their capacity to grieve is utterly real and when they *can* regard us as unique in the more rudimentary but important sense captured by the words "Nobody else will do".

Can we love strangers?

I am not pessimistic about love in general, nor about the possibility of a genuine love for non-human animals, nor about the possibility of love for non-sentient life forms and for natural environments of various sorts. Pessimism about the nature of love for the non-human does not strike me as more helpful or more realistic than pessimism about the nature of sexualized intimate love. Such love for the non-human may also, up to a point, be understood in the light of our experience of the latter. What I am doubtful about is the very idea of love for strangers. I do not deny the possibility that we may love our neighbours in the way that Christians consider admirable and important, even though I do not uncritically share such admiration. But I do not believe that love of this sort can be extended "all the way out" so that it allows for the possibility of loving those with whom we have no prior familiarity. Loving someone like Diana or Pope John Paul is a rather different matter. However we understand our relation to them, they are not unknown to us.

Put in more concrete terms, I want to suggest that we cannot, in any straightforward sense, love anyone on our first meeting, when we bump into them for the first time in the street, or on a train or at some social function. What leads me to draw the bounds of love in this way is, again, an appreciation of the limits of grief. We cannot love strangers in any straightforward sense because we cannot grieve for them. And our inability to do so is *not* a moral failing. It is an upshot of the nature of grief. Even Jesus, the Buddha or Socrates could not grieve for a stranger. We can and often do feel sorrow and pity upon the death of those we do not know. It is saddening to see the body of an unknown motorcyclist by the side of the road, and we need not feel indifferent or guilty about any imagined lack of care. But if the account of grief and of false grief that I have set out above is broadly correct, we cannot grieve for them in any genuine sense. In the absence of a prior history of care and concern, apparent grief could only be an instance of false grief.

I am not suggesting that we lack *any* history of connection to strangers. Taken far enough back, everything shares a history with everything else. Humans, as part of a shared human community, are connected to one another in ways that go beyond the sharing of our biological and physical origins. But a shared history of this sort is very different from the shared history of lovers and family, friends and neighbours. It is a shared history that does not require intimacy, and without intimacy, without a concern for the other having worked its way into the fibre of our being, grief seems inconceivable. I am also not implying that the hospital or prison visitor who is inspired by Christian ideals cannot, over time, come to love those they visit. I am simply suggesting that they cannot do so instantly, in a voluntaristic manner or at first glance. Even so, given the peculiarity of such circumstances, and the fact that the person who is visited happens to be exposed in an unusually vulnerable way, they may quickly cease to be a stranger and love of a sort may then become possible. Once they are known, and once there is some history of care, they can be loved and an indication that they can be loved is that their loss may be an occasion for genuine grief.

My scepticism about the genuineness of love for strangers also does not involve doubt about our having obligations towards them: obligations, for example, to welcome the stranger in our midst or even to show compassion towards them. But accepting this is very different from saying, "We ought to love strangers", or at least it is very different if this claim is understood in a literal sense. If all that is meant is "We ought to show hospitality and be nice to strangers", then I have no objection at all. We can, do and ought to care for strangers in various ways. Genuine hospitality is a remarkable and beautiful thing but it is unhelpful to call it love. Instead of enriching our conceptual repertoire, such a move would tend to diminish it by equating "love" and "care".

I care (or at least I believe that I care) for neighbours and acquaintances and I do try to be welcoming towards those I do not know. Sometimes I feel sorrow for their hardships and, occasionally, anger about their mistreatment. But this is care of a sort that should not be confused with love. We humans have a complex emotional repertoire and a wide range of concepts that help us to make sense of our lives. We need to preserve our concepts in all their distinctiveness if we are to have a sufficiently rich picture of what it is like to be human. In line with this, we may say that *loving* does involve *caring* but not every kind of care is an instance of love. I have taken it that when we talk about love, what we are concerned with is care of a particularly robust sort or, more precisely, care of a special, deep and, in a sense, intimate sort. The way in which I have tried to make sense of this kind of caring is by claiming that it is care in which we invest our own personal contentment. Accordingly, when we love, our happiness is conditional on what happens to the unique and irreplaceable other that we happen to love. And when things go badly, when the worst happens, we grieve.

By contrast with "love for strangers", talk about "love for humanity" need not be figurative or misleading. There may be a real sense in which we can love mankind, or (in less gendered terms) humanity, just so long as doing so is not taken to involve loving *all* the particular individuals who go to make it up. Instead, such love concerns "our group", that is, a particular interbreeding population and its offspring. This is very different from loving a biological species or loving something abstract such as a "human type". After all, the currently existing humans could, with a single exception, be killed off and then replaced by a different and unrelated set of humans. We might even imagine such a wholesale replacement as the outcome of a second creation, carried out to replace the earlier botched job. Under such circumstances, the last survivor of the original batch could grieve over the loss of her group, and such grief need not be about any particular individual. Still less need it be grief about the loss of a species, or a type of creature. Creatures of the same species and type would still be around.

Because I reject the possibility of love without the *right kind* of shared history, I am also committed to rejecting any literal account of "love at first sight". That too would involve a special instance of love for a stranger. But I am only rejecting the idea that love can suddenly spring into existence, fully formed. I do not reject the idea that there can be an unusual experience or a cluster of unusual experiences when we first meet someone whom we later go on to love. And love itself can begin to grow very quickly. Some of the components of a fully fledged love can even be put in place at speed, but not all of them. The pattern of desires that love involves is always slower to mature. Desires for the well-being of another person can only become entangled with an everyday concern for our own well-being over the course of time. It does not happen instantaneously.

Nonetheless, love must start somewhere and we can *begin* the process even with a stranger. That is to say, *falling in love* can begin in a moment and it can begin not in spite of the fact that the other person is a stranger but because of it, because we do not guard against them in the way that we guard ourselves against those we know. Eric Fromm writes in *The Art of Loving* (1956) about the experience of encountering someone in this way:

> If two people who have been strangers, as all of us are, suddenly let the wall between them break down, and feel close, feel one, this moment of oneness is one of the most exhilarating, most exciting experiences in life. It is all the more wonderful and miraculous for persons who have been shut off, isolated, without love. (2000: 4)

But even Fromm distinguishes between *falling in love* and *standing in love*, which presupposes a closer and shared history.

Falling in love is a process that can begin in a moment but can only be completed if the other person ceases to be a stranger. We can, at a first meeting, see or believe that "Here is someone with whom I could live a wonderful life" or "Here is someone I could care for deeply and who might care for me in return". But this is only a starting-point. If my memory serves me well, I recall feeling this way about Suzanne on the occasion when we first met in the 1980s, at a less-than-glamorous location. It was a strange experience, difficult to describe accurately and honestly in retrospect. Perhaps it involved the sudden onset of a kind of longing or the awareness of a previously unnoticed desire. Perhaps things of this sort happen all the time, to someone somewhere. But saying this is different from holding that these initial stirrings of love are ever the fully formed item.

Love for the natural

I have already accepted that a form of love may be possible for some non-sentient and even inanimate entities. This commitment helps to situate the bounds of love in such an expansive way that other life forms, and living systems with which we are familiar, will fall well within the territory of what we can love. And so they do. This is a circumstance that will be all the more striking if it turns out to be the case that there are some humans, that is, strangers, whom we cannot love. When it comes to love, familiarity will then be more important than personhood.

For simplicity, and because "love for the non-human and non-sentient but living natural" is somewhat cumbersome, I shall refer instead to "love for the natural". The idea of such love is not new. Plato alludes to it in the *Phaedrus* and writes about it directly in the *Laws*. In both instances he shows a strong sense of connection to what is familiar and close at hand, at one point suggesting that we should cherish the land more than any child or mother because it is a goddess and "mistress of mortal men" (*Laws* 740a). The gods and spirits of the locality are also to be treated in the same way. Even in our own times, when gods and spirits rarely figure, and when land and place are often regarded as exchangeable commodities, there have always been dissenting voices that have held out for an approach that involves love. The best known of these voices belongs to Aldo Leopold. His pioneering mid-twentieth-century case for environmentalism, *A Sand County Almanac* (1949), argues that we need a land ethic and that "We can be ethical only in relation to something we can see, feel, understand, love, or otherwise have faith in" (1968: 214). There remains, in Leopold, a tension between a concern for land and a concern for animals, together with a tension between love of nature in general and an implied and far more personal connection to particular things and places. Even so, we may readily appreciate his reasons for appealing to love. Any of us can come to care for woodlands, forests and mountains in a deep way that ties our well-being to their fortunes.

Upon the destruction of some cared-for place, grief, or something akin to grief, is a genuine possibility. The botanist Phyllis Windle makes this point in her short essay "The Ecology of Grief" (1992). Windle calls on her experience as a hospital chaplain as well as her familiarity with the reactions of fellow scientists to the loss of the species, habitats and wilderness that they have studied, and to whose fortunes their own well-being has become tied in a way that fits poorly with their self image as objective and detached:

> We have almost no social support for expressing this grief. When I sit beside a hospital bed as a chaplain, I expect people to cry about the unwelcome changes they are experiencing. I expect and accept patients' feelings that are dark and intense … Honest conversations about grief that come quite naturally at a bedside are far more difficult at a lab bench or conference table.
> (1992: 365)

To set the loss of a loved human and the loss of something non-sentient side by side may strike some people as implausible. It is tempting to ask, "Can we really care for an area of land or of ancient (or just plain old) woodland in this way?" I suppose it is harder to do so now than at almost any other time in the past. Many of us (myself included) live in ways that are far removed from contact with whatever sits outside buildings and beyond streets. But there have always been those whose sense of connection to place is stronger. Drive them off the land and they no longer feel themselves to be the same beings. Indigenous peoples who are cleared in the name of improvement would be a good example here. But if we can speak of their grief at the loss of some natural place, or upon the loss of some living but non-sentient thing, the love that is the source of this grief may turn out to be love of a special and interesting sort. At first blush, love for the natural seems entirely unlike sexualized intimate love. It may be all very well for the ecologically minded to follow Leopold (1968: 129) and to say that we ought to try "Thinking Like a Mountain", but I am pretty sure that mountains do not think and that such comments are not meant to be taken literally. Nor do mountains, woodland and forests desire our flourishing or desire to prevent harm to us in the way that a lover or a sentient companion animal may do. Least of all do mountains have such a desire in a way that is bound up with desires for their own well-being. In brief, any love we have for the natural must surely be unreciprocated, and this may make it seem curiously akin to a gift, just as Christian love is sometimes spoken of as a gift. It is a gratuitous or one-sided response to that which we live alongside. Alternatively, we may be inclined to suspect that such love is a petty drama played out entirely within the self.

This impression of one-sidedness may be misleading. At least sometimes, love for a life-filled place involves a personal connection that sets it apart from all other places. It involves ties that *bind* us here but not elsewhere. This may be more obvious in the case of the loved places of our youth, which is a time when exploration takes on a tangible and expansive dimension. But because it involves such a personal connection, the similarity to a kind of gift-love, rather than a love that binds, is slight. It may also be misleading to say, without qualification, that there can be no reciprocation *in any sense*. It is true that woodlands and valleys and familiar well-trodden places in the hills cannot love us back in the way that a spouse, partner or lover may, but they can, if only figuratively, give us something in return. Put crudely, we can benefit from the experiences that such a love brings into our lives, the experiences it involves and makes possible. And this takes us away from the idea that the love in question is utterly one-sided, or that it is a private fantasy or an absolute gift. It points instead to the idea that such love may have significant similarities to sexualized intimate love when the latter is reciprocated. Like the latter, such a love can be a source of calm pleasure or joy. It may even be a source of the special kind of joy that we experience with the whole of our being.

There is still a danger of romanticizing love for the natural and, in the process, losing sight of the ethical indifference of nature: its indifference to how we or anyone else may feel. Nature is both a source of great good and, simultaneously, the enabler of great suffering and harm. Living things exist through the possibilities that each open up to the other, but often they exist at each other's expense. The natural world is not a place where there is any stable and benevolent equilibrium. But to point this out need not drive us towards a different kind of romanticism that loses sight of all that is good, focuses only on harshness and then finds it beautiful. It is not unknown for individuals to reflect, "Nature doesn't worry about rules and the weak, so why should we?" But this is still a romanticized ethic, albeit of a more specialized sort, lapsing as it does into the fantasy that we are in some way comparable to inconceivably greater forces.

An alternative to the romanticization of the natural need not involve stripping the non-sentient of all value and importance, or the denial that we can have a truly deep and loving connection to it, or at least a truly deep and loving connection to some portions of the natural world with which we are familiar. It need not involve a refusal to accept the reality of grief in the face of loss (denial of the sort that worries Windle). Love of a place and the loss of a place are experiences that are both familiar and difficult to ignore. They can form part of our experience. Alternatively, they can be seen at a distance, as they are represented in books, films and other narratives. Here, I am tempted to mention a small part of the life that is shared by Suzanne and myself. We never tire of watching *Local Hero* (1983), a smallish-budget film that is set in a part of Scotland so far to the north that when you look out at the sea it is as if you stand on the edge of the world. In the film, an old beachcomber is offered money to allow the development of the beach that he, by a quirk of history, happens to own. He enjoys himself a good deal at the expense of the developer's agents. They cannot understand that there is no right price, not even a big one. Love for the shore that he works is part of the fibre of his being. Selling it is not an option. No amount of money will do: not even a bucketful of cash that would allow him to buy another and different beach in a warmer and easier place. After all, it wouldn't be the same beach.

I can understand this strong attachment to place even though the places that I was attached to in my own youth are now largely gone. No obstinate man stood in the way of developers, although one of my childhood neighbours would perhaps have done so, given half a chance. He was a man in his nineties when my own years were still numbered in single figures. Before the war he had farmed most of the land that the village now sat on and he knew what lay beneath: the underground streams, the dried-up river beds and the places where animals would rest while sheltering from the sun or rain. Forced into a compulsory purchase, he found himself with money that he never used. Instead, he stayed on in one of the newly built council houses situated close to a filled-in stream that had once run down from a nearby hill where the local barns had stood, protecting the grain on high ground. Looking back, I can make sense of the idea that he loved this small piece of land and that, even when it had been cleared of almost all that he once cared for, he still could not bear to part from it.

I cite his case because it is so different from my own, and between us we give some idea of the range of human responsiveness. As matters stand, I would not say that I love any local portion of the natural world. While some kinds of damage and destruction make me sad or angry or sometimes both, I am still inclined to think that there is no wooded area or wilderness, hill, glen or valley whose loss would cause me to grieve in the way that I have seen others grieve. Perhaps I am wrong about this, and perhaps I do love some favoured place, somewhere along the seashore, or a hidden grove or one of the woodland areas that Suzanne and I intermittently visit. But I might not be wrong. Things may be just as they appear. My love may always be directed elsewhere. Even so, I can appreciate that under the right circumstances I could come to love such a place and that doing so might be healthy in a more-than-medical sense. I do not regard the absence of such love on my part as the achievement of a desirable objectivity. I regard it as a shortcoming that is all too familiar and understandable given the way most of us now live.

By drawing attention to my own case I allude to a broader suspicion that the absence of love for the natural can be bad for us. The loss of places that we can readily love, and the loss of those connections to the rest of the natural world that would allow us to do so, can be detrimental to human relations. More specifically, I want to suggest that we now love far too few things or too small a range of things with the upshot that sexualized intimate love between persons, and perhaps also the love of parents for their children, can be left to carry too great a burden. It is, after all, no easy or simple thing for those we love, and who love us in return, if all of our most important hopes and aspirations come to depend exclusively upon them. It can be hard for anyone to bear the full brunt of another's undivided love and perhaps unfair to expect them to do so. But the solution to this problem is the expansion of our love towards more of those things that we can love, rather than its withdrawal or curtailment.

Further reading

Plato's dialogues the *Symposium* and the *Phaedrus* remain the most important contributions to our understanding of love. They are also an excellent starting-point for those who wish to read further. For the connection between love and the recognition of value, Raimond Gaita's *Our Common Humanity* (2002) is an extremely readable volume. The second edition of his *Good and Evil* (2004) also covers the same territory but in a more philosophically demanding way.

For criticisms of the idea of love as union a good place to look is Irving Singer's *Philosophy of Love* (2009), which will also direct you to Singer's more substantial contributions to our understanding of love. Alan Soble's *The Philosophy of Sex and Love* (2008) provides a more hardcore analytic criticism of union accounts as well as an excellent critical overview of a series of familiar claims about love. If you get hold of a copy make sure it's the (significantly expanded) second edition.

For discussion of what we can love and grieve over, see Phyllis Windle's classic essay on ecological loss "The Ecology of Grief" (1992) and, for the love of animals, see my *Beyond Animal Rights* (2010). For irreplaceability as a built-in feature of an enriched concept of pethood, see my "Dependent Companions" (2009).

On a more localized note, current academic discussions of the philosophy of love presuppose familiarity with David Velleman's "Love as a Moral Emotion" (1999), Niko Kolodny's "Love as Valuing a Relationship" (2003) and Harry Frankfurt's *The Reasons of Love* (2004). These works help to set the overall context for discussions about irreplaceability and for the disputed idea that we can have reasons for love. Velleman and Kolodny support the idea while Frankfurt rejects it. Bennett Helm's impressive, scholarly and challenging volume *Love, Friendship and the Self* (2010) appeared as I was writing this book, and promises to be one of the dominant features on the landscape for years to come.

References

Benedict [1996] 2006. *Deus Caritas Est*. San Francisco: St Ingnatius Press.

Bowlby, J. 1951. *Maternal Care and Mental Health*. Geneva: World Health Organization.

Dostoyevsky, F. [1866] 2000. *Crime and Punishment*, C. Garnett (trans.). Ware: Wordsworth.

Freud, S. 1984. *On Sexuality: Three Essays on the Theory of Sexuality and Other Works*, J. Strachey (trans.). Harmondsworth: Penguin.

Frankfurt, H. G. 2004. *The Reasons of Love*. Princeton, NJ: Princeton University Press.

Fromm, E. [1956] 2000. *The Art of Loving*. New York: HarperCollins.

Gaita, R. 2002. *Our Common Humanity*. London: Routledge.

Gaita, R. 2004. *Good and Evil: An Absolute Conception*, 2nd edn. London: Routledge.

Gutmann, A. & D. Thompson 1996. *Democracy and Disagreement*. Cambridge, MA: Harvard University Press.

Helm, B. 2010. *Love, Friendship and the Self*. Oxford: Oxford University Press.

Joyce, J. [1914] 1992. *The Dubliners*. Harmondsworth: Penguin.

à Kempis, T. [*c*.1418–27] 1952. *The Imitation of Christ*, L. Sherley-Price (trans.). Harmondsworth: Penguin.

Kierkegaard, S. [1847] 2009. *Works of Love*, H. Hong & E. Hong (trans.). New York: Harper Perennial.

Kolodny, N. 2003. "Love as Valuing a Relationship". *Philosophical Review* **112**(2): 135–89.

Lewis, C. S. 1964. *The Four Loves*. London: Collins.

Lem, S. 2003. *Solaris*, J. Kilmartin & S. Cox (trans.). London: Faber.

Leopold, A. [1949] 1968. *A Sand County Almanac*. Oxford: Oxford University Press.

Margolies, L. 1999. "The Long Good-bye: Women, Companion Animals and Maternal Loss". *Clinical Social Work Journal* **27**(3): 289–304.

Midgley, M. 1983. *Animals and Why They Matter*. Athens, GA: University of Georgia Press.

Milligan, T. 2007. "Murdochian Humility". *Religious Studies* **43**(2): 217–28.

Milligan, T. 2008. "False Emotions". *Philosophy* **83**(2): 213–30.

Milligan, T. 2009. "Dependent Companions". *Journal of Applied Ethics* **26**(4): 402–13.

Milligan, T. 2010. *Beyond Animal Rights*. London: Continuum.

Milton, J. [1667] 2004. *Paradise Lost*, S. Orgel & J. Goldberg (eds). Oxford: Oxford University Press.

Murdoch, I. 1969. *Bruno's Dream*. London: Chatto & Windus.

Murdoch, I. 1999. *Existentialists and Mystics*, P. Conradi (ed.). Harmondsworth: Penguin.

Nietzsche, F. 1986. *Thus Spoke Zarathustra*, R. J. Hollingdale (trans.). Harmondsworth: Penguin.

Nygren, A. [1932–39] 1969. *Agape and Eros*, P. S. Watson (trans.). New York: Harper & Row.

Parfit, D. [1984] 1992. *Reasons and Persons*. Oxford: Oxford University Press.

Pitcher, G. 1996. *The Dogs who Came to Stay*. New York: Plume.

Plato 1980. *The Republic*, A. D. Lindsay (trans.). London: Everyman.

Plato 1984. *The Laws*, T. J. Saunders (trans.). Harmondsworth: Penguin.

Plato 2000. *The Symposium*, C. Gill (trans.). London: Penguin.

Plato 2005a. *Meno and Other Dialogues*, R. Waterfield (trans.). Oxford: Oxford University Press.

Plato, 2005b. *Phaedrus*, C. Rowe (trans.). London: Penguin.

Proust, M. 2002. *Swann's Way*, C. K. Scott Moncrieff & T. Kilmartin (trans.). London: Vintage.

Schopenhauer, A. 1958. *The World as Will and Representation*, E. Payne (trans.), 3 vols. Indian Hills, CO: Falcon's Wing Press.

Schopenhauer, A. 1970. *Essays and Aphorisms*, R. J. Hollingdale (trans.). London: Penguin.

Seneca. 1977. *Letters from a Stoic*, R. Campbell (trans.). Harmondsworth: Penguin.

Singer, I. 2009. *Philosophy of Love: A Partial Summing-Up*. Cambridge, MA: MIT Press.

Soble, A. 2008. *The Philosophy of Sex and Love*, 2nd edn. Minnesota: Paragon House.

Soskice, J. 1992. "Love and Attention". In *Philosophy, Religion and the Spiritual Life*, M. McGhee (ed.). Royal Institute of Philosophy Supplement, **32**.

Stendhal [1822] 1975. *Love*, G. Sale & S. Sale (trans.). Harmondsworth: Penguin.

Stendhal [1830] 1977. *Scarlet and Black*, M. R. B. Shaw (trans.). Harmondsworth: Penguin.

Velleman, D. 1999. "Love as a Moral Emotion". *Ethics* **109**(2): 338–74.

Weil, S. 1951. *Waiting for God*, E. Crawford (trans.). London: Routledge.

Weil, S. 1952. *The Need for Roots*, A. Wills (trans.). London: Routledge.

Windle, P. 1992. "The Ecology of Grief". *Bioscience* **42**(5): 363–6.

Index

agape 9, 61–2, 68
Aquinas, Thomas 44, 64
Aristotle 58
attention 1, 52–3, 119
authority 53

Benedict, Pope 68
bereavement 89–91
betrayal 93
Bowlby, John 14, 27
Buddhism 19

caritas 9
Christian love 5, 15, 57–72
companion animals 127, 134; *see
also* pets
compassion 41, 43
conditional desires 91–2, 117

Dante 37, 44
death 87, 92
duplicates 99, 102–4, 124

egocentricity 31, 41, 44, 52–3, 59
eros 9, 58, 61, 68, 75

false grief 122–3, 128
fools 19, 33; *see also* folly
folly 23, 29, 36, 49; *see also* fools
Frankfurt, Harry 41
Freud, Sigmund 4, 14, 21–3, 27, 35,
58, 65–6, 77, 103, 117
friends 59, 117
Fromm, Eric 131

Gaita, Raimond 51–2, 56, 58, 61,
71

happiness 33, 40, 48, 80

infancy 27
intimacy 80, 97, 108

joy 1, 9, 25, 48, 135
Joyce, James 16–17, 113–14

Kant, Immanuel 53
Kierkegaard, Søren 30–31, 35, 39,
69–71
knowledge 109–15

Lem, Stanislaw 102–4
Leopold, Aldo 133–4
Lewis, C. S. 68
libido 58, 66
liebestod 92
longing 1, 9, 43, 77
love at first sight 7, 130–32

mental illness 89, 93
Midgley, Mary 36
Milton, John 44
mixed intentionality 25–7, 70, 126
Murdoch, Iris 37, 55–8, 72

narcissistic love 21–2
narratives 32, 60
Nietzsche, Friedrich 42, 88, 117
Nygren, Anders 5, 61, 63–6, 69–71

openness (to love) 4, 46
overestimation 26, 95

parental love 2, 9, 12, 14, 52, 58, 61,
71, 117–18, 134

Parfit, Derek   98–101, 104, 106
Paul, St   61–2
pessimism about the nature of love
      2–5, 8–13, 16–17, 24, 32–3, 45, 57,
      70, 109
pets   18, 124–6; *see also* companion
      animals
philia   9, 62; *see also* friends
pity   41–3
Plato   31, 39–40, 44, 58, 69, 81, 105,
      117
   Laws   132
   Lysis   13–14
   Phaedrus   76, 132
   Symposium   37–8, 75
Proust, Marcel   4, 21, 23, 27, 35, 77,
      103

romanticism   92

scepticism about being loved   3, 4, 11,
      13, 17, 24, 57, 110–12
Schopenhauer, Arthur   4, 18–23,
      32–5, 40–43, 47, 49
self-doubt   49

Seneca   97–9
sex   6, 72, 79–80, 92, 108, 116
Shakespeare, William   29, 32, 107–8
Singer, Irving   82–3
Stendhal   34, 35, 40–41, 44

Titian   66–7
trust   83–4

union   81–2

value   4, 45, 48–9, 51–3, 57, 63–5; *see
      also* worth
vegetarianism   85–6
Velleman, David   79
Virgil   37, 42
virtue   58, 64
vulnerability   80, 90, 98, 129

Weil, Simone   69
well-being   6, 34, 43, 73, 80, 92–3,
      116–17, 119, 127
Windle, Phylis   133, 136
worth   45–6, 48–9, 51, 54, 57, 63, 65;
      see also value